PRAISE for Lost Man Found

"*What a story! It was compelling from beginning to end. I do think it's a page turner. And his recovery is powerfully conveyed. It serves as a great example to all of us that lives can be turned around.*"

– Karen Casey,
author of *Each Day a New Beginning*

"*What a moving account, unsparingly candid, of a man turning from darkness to light. May Sam's story help those also struggling to know that love and peace are possible, even for the very lost.*"

– Fr. Richard Rohr,
author of *Falling Upward,
Spirituality for the Two Halves of Life*

"Like me, Sam is a person with a troubled life. When I was a kid, I pulled away into myself, too. I shunned religion also, because there was no forgiving, and I was going to hell anyhow. I wish someone had talked to me and told me my way of thinking wasn't right. To change, you need to know what makes you operate and why you did the things you did so it won't happen again. Sam figured that out."

– Marshall,
served 31 years in prison for
first degree murder

"Sam is a lovely man, and I thank him for giving us his story. If an impulsive, alcoholic, traumatized, Vietnam veteran child molester raised in a barren home can find God, selflessness, and peace, there is hope for all of us and no excuse for most of us."

– District Court Judge Bruce Peterson,
co-founder with Elissa Hulin Peterson of
The Sullivan Ballou Fund

LOST MAN FOUND

*Crime, punishment &
growing a soul*

by **KARIN WINEGAR**
& MICHAEL A. RICCI, JR.

HORSE FEED PRESS

Lost Man Found
Crime, Punishment & Growing a Soul
By Karin Winegar
& Michael A. Ricci, Jr.

Copyright 2019 Michael A. Ricci, Jr.

Library of Congress 2018912380
Published in the United States by
Horse Feed Press.

HORSE FEED PRESS

Horse Feed Press ISBN: 978-0-692-11407-0
For more on Horse Feed Press please visit
www.karinwinegar.com
Book design by Joan Nygren
Printed in the United States of America

ALSO BY KARIN WINEGAR

Public Works

Fire and Spice, The Cuisine of Sri Lanka

*SAVED, Rescued Animals and
The Lives They Transform*

Tina of Grand Avenue

Commissioned Private Works

*Never Stop Dreaming,
The Gus Schickedanz Story*

*High Expectations,
The Doug Leatherdale Story*

CONTENTS

The events and the narrator of this book are real, however, names and locations have been changed to protect privacy.

Not until we are lost
do we begin to understand ourselves.
∼ Henry David Thoreau

The Door Is Always Open

"Within about a 96-hour period of time, I got to Vietnam, inhaled my first cigarette, got drunk for the very first time, had my 19th birthday, and shot and killed my first two human beings. I liked all of it."

I am here to meet this speaker, a man who has by any standard led a troubled life, who has hurt and been hurt, and who has over many years with the assistance of steadfast willpower, luck and various help, survived and reached redemption.

Or rather, as Sam might say, is in the process of it.

The front door of Sam's revitalized suburban-style 1960s rambler stands open wide. The storm door reflects the images of tractor trailers, 18-wheelers, and yellow and green John Deere farm implements whooshing up and down the asphalt on the grade beyond a rank of infant lilac bushes. As I stood on the sunlit stoop, a warm baritone voice came from the shadows across the room: "I have one rule in this house for all — just walk in and holler. No door bell, don't knock. Whether I am here or not, all are welcome."

Sam came out of prison the last time sporting a full white beard and ponytail. This mid-summer morning his silver hair is cut short, his salt and pepper mustache is trim, and his jaw and chin carry a two- or three-day stubble.

Behind brown-rimmed bifocals, whites visible on the circumference of his large blue eyes give him a look of astonishment, perhaps shock. The sleeves of his faded work shirt are rolled to show still-powerful forearms, the remains of the husky man he once was. His left elbow is swollen to baseball size with bursitis above thin white scars, the legacy of falling onto punji sticks in Vietnam.

Military service pins glitter on his tired dark blue baseball cap, its bill crimped and greasy. More medals, framed in walnut on burgundy velvet, perch atop a bookcase: the Purple Heart, a silver star, an oak leaf cluster, three bronze stars, a Vietnamese Cross of Gallantry, and the colorful bars worn in place of medals on less formal occasions.

Everything is clean, not sparse, but tightly ordered, the style of a lone man accustomed to making a functional home in a constricted space.

I notice he carries a clear plastic coffee mug, a prison-issue relic, Sam tells me, decorated with a mother polar bear and her cubs, deeply scratched and stained tobacco-brown at the rim.

We walk past a copy of 1 Corinthians 13:13 ("The greatest of these is love") in a gilt frame on the wall at the front door and down the hall to his office, a converted bedroom at the rear of the split-level house.

A faux granite countertop set atop on file cabinets against one wall serves as work surface. Its shelves hold a fat roll of postage stamps taped on an unfolded paper clip, bowls of wrapped Life Savers and hard caramels, a pack of L & M cigarettes, copies of *Grapevine*, the 12 Step magazine, and, incongruously to me, a jar of pickled pepperoncini. My habit as a longtime newspaper reporter is to snoop shamelessly and openly, and so near a clipping of the Prayer of St. Francis, I spot a cluster of prescription bottles from the Veterans' Administration pharmacy lashed together with rubber bands.

Among the stack of CDs are Vivaldi, Kitaro, Gordon Lightfoot, and Willie Nelson—I am surprised at the mix, which is like my own eclectic taste in music. Sam's possessions are already throwing me off any preconceptions I had about someone who has served time in prison.

Among the well-thumbed books I see more familiar faces: *The Essential Gandhi, Around the Year With Emmett Fox, The Buddha*, and *Zen*. Sam, however, takes a more intense approach to his reading matter than I do. His copy of the recovery classic *24 Hours a Day* riffles with hundreds of turquoise, pink, coral, and lime green Post-Its. Passages are underlined and shot through with orange highlights, up to three sizzling colors in one paragraph. This is an intense, perhaps even desperate person, I think to myself.

A bundle of the smallest, most worn paperbacks — *The Best of Bill, The Little Red Book, Twelve Steps and Twelve Traditions* — is held tightly by four rubber bands. This appears to be his life preserver, a spiritual recovery kit clutched through many hours, many meetings, and, I surmise, through considerable internal agony.

What Sam mostly reads now are three newspapers a day — two regional dailies and *The New York Times*, where he does the Sunday crossword "in ink" he says, with a knowing look at me.

The office contains as well a printer-copier, but the usual computer that links to them is absent. Sam says he has never allowed himself to have one. There are people he doesn't want to find him and people he is not ready to find, face, or follow.

"I've led a life of destruction, and I found a path to salvation," says Sam. "And along the way, I realized there is not enough love."

I am here to discover and write about how that life unfolded from what Sam says was his internal anarchy and his external evils to, many years on, a hard-won form of peace.

"Peace is not the absence of trouble but

rather the presence of a higher power, a spiritual response rather than the human-based one," he says. "Christ and Buddha — real pains in the ass, you know? Who the hell wants to turn the other cheek? Change is good — you go first," he chuckles.

As we talk, Sam alternates smoking with puffs on a lung moisturizing machine kept close to hand atop a wicker cart in his office. Decades of steady smoking have cost him lung function and occasionally landed him in the emergency room and hospital. When he does smoke, it is outdoors on his back deck and considerately downwind from nonsmoking visitors such as me.

Against the living room wall, shelves display a collection of frilly china music boxes — shepherdesses, clowns, frothy skaters, glittering faeries, carousel horses, a glossy street car. Model tall ships sail on a ledge near the kitchen, where the counter holds a significant stack of empty ice cream buckets. On a table facing the balcony and backyard beyond, pink hibiscus blossoms are drying next to a jigsaw puzzle — the deadly slow garden image type.

"That's for practicing patience," says Sam, "something I never had most of my life."

We step through the glass balcony door out onto the deck overlooking a steep, shady slope. Below us, chickadees peep and bounce, cardinals and orioles flash by, and warblers dive among a dozen feeders offering seeds and grape jelly.

"There were so many prices paid by so many to grow my soul," he says, smoking and leaning on the railing to contemplate the feeding flock. "Sometimes I just come out here and say, 'Thank you, God.'"

Sam is paying his own, self-imposed price. From his home he mails hand-printed letters to friends, some still in prison, and to their families. He stuffs the envelopes with copies of cartoons, adages, newspaper clippings, and his thoughts. He estimates some 40,000 pages have passed through his five-year old copier.

"I send about 1,100 letters a year; my record for the most letters written in one year is 1,900," he tells me.

Across from his desk, ranging from floor to ceiling, are a dozen shelves of books and plastic storage boxes labeled Rehab, Religion, Dirt, Toons. Some shelves are buckling under the weight of numerous white three-ring binders. The books on these shelves are a fragmentary relic of the 806 books he read while in five prisons. For everything he read, Sam kept a literary log printed in neat capital letters noting the year read, the number of pages in each book, and rating each with stars, the odd smiley face or the occasional "Ugh!"

He is impressively and widely well-read—again shattering my expectations. Through the years, he steamed on from *Mein Kampf* to Dostoyevsky, Reinhold Niebuhr to Shel Silverstein, all of Forsyth's *Hornblower* series, Robert Ludlum, *The Iliad*, and Louis L'Amour.

He took on Plutarch, Voltaire (10 stars and an exclamation point for *Candide*) and Herman Hesse, William Faulkner, John Cheever and James Michener. He delved into Thucydides' *Peloponnesian War* and Bertrand Russell's *Why I Am Not a Christian* (which earned a 'Wow' as well as stars and underlines.) He did not hesitate to read all of Jane Austen or Winston Churchill's 466-page *History of the English People*. Sam gave eleven stars to both Joseph Campbell's *The Power of Myth* and Michael Newton's *Journey of Souls*. Thomas Moore's *Care of the Soul* was awarded 10 stars, while sad faces mark the listings for books by Sidney Sheldon, Ken Follett, and Diana Ross.

As a fellow bookworm, I found myself internally cheering both his taste and his rating system. This man has discipline, I thought, or motivation or both. He obviously had the time, but who knew that at least some prison libraries contain the literary classics?

Right in the middle of 829 pages of *A Sense*

of History, he noted in his book log "Lockdown week, all library books taken, RATS BAH HUMBUG." That made me wonder what possible harm such books could pose to anyone, and worse, what is there to do in prison without books?

The Shack, a fictional novel about the kidnapping and murder of a child and her father's subsequent encounter with the Holy Trinity, is one of Sam's chief inspirations. "Have the tissues handy when you read it," he advises.

In his reading log, on the line for *Conversations with God* by Neale Donald Walsch, he wrote "Top Book of all time." Years earlier in this log, he had declared Mark Twain's *The Mysterious Stranger* "#1 All Time Best." When he was released from the last prison, after serving 10 years of a 15-year sentence, he was reading Patricia Hampl's *Virgin Time*.

Books did not keep him content to be in prison, I was to learn, but the almost monkish life he chose to lead inside gave him the freedom from distractions and temptations. In what may be an act unique to Sam, he begged to serve the additional five years and was refused. He currently has a couple of years of what convicts call "paper" — supervised parole — to go.

There are episodes from Sam's prison time that cannot be shared in order to protect men still incarcerated. Suffice it to say, he had very close calls, and criminal behavior continues on the inside that can fatally affect those on the outside, too.

Prison time, books, certain friends in low places and others in high moral places, the spiritual practices of 12 Step recovery, and severe self-examination explain how he became what he is today. We share coffee from the green metal thermos on his desk (he has bought milk for mine) sit almost knee to knee, and I aim the recorder at him and listen. When he went into prison, Sam admits, he was a predator, a man without a conscience.

"My emotional IQ was locked at zero and had been for years," he recalls. "For decades I was child-like, acting out mentally, verbally, and physically as my expectations were not met. Prisons are full of millions of us. So are bars, slums, crack houses, meth dens."

He passes me a stiff, slightly yellow paper, a page of the script from the film *The Green Mile*. Through repeated viewings Sam has captured part of the movie dialogue. Set in a Southern prison during the Depression, the film centers on John Coffey, an outsized inmate with psychic and empathic abilities who forms a friendship with Paul, a death row prison officer played by Tom Hanks.

"John talks about the needles inside his head, how he can feel others' suffering," Sam said. A tear hits his cheek, skirts his glasses and bounces to his grey t-shirt worn beneath an unbuttoned blue work shirt. "I have an awareness now of the pain of other people because of my own. I'm done causing pain to people,

I don't have the stomach to do the pain anymore. I'm done with the anger and the hate."

Sam coughs long and wetly, puffs on his lung medication, chews the edge of his mustache, and I begin to find out how the door to his heart slammed shut. I will learn how he became what he was, about the consequences to him and to others, about a monumental effort to change and a rare redemption. I will uncover what it took to open that door — and all doors — again.

— Karin Winegar

LOST

ONE

Walking with Lions

Sam learned and did things in Vietnam as at no other time in his life — fear, for one, brotherhood, for another, killing for a third. He began to see who he was and what he wasn't and, in relating this to me, he was perfectly candid.

This is not a war story. This is a story about a man who had no feelings for other people and how he became that way. How he hurt women and a child and how he treated other men. How that changed, and how, against the odds, he changed. It did not start in Vietnam, but perhaps because of the public drama of the times it expressed itself there very clearly, perhaps most clearly. And so very early: he was 19 and 20 during his military service. The other crimes were more secret, more private and took place later. So this is a cautionary warning from Sam and from me.

In 1967 through 1969 he was one of more than 485,000 U.S. troops stationed in Vietnam engaged in a war started under false pretexts, waged for uncertain reasons and one that could not be won.

"'Nam was not the issue," he wrote me in one of his letters spattered with copies of newspaper cartoons. "It was near total lack of a sense of horror, compassion, empathy. Damn near impossible to describe how little conscience existed and instant burial of it when it popped up.

"In May '67, I arrived in Vietnam, six others and I reported to our company headquarters at An Khê, and that night I got drunk for the first time in my life. Back home, during holiday dinners at grandmother's house, I'd had a small glass of Mogen David and found I didn't like alcohol. I didn't even know the name of drinks or beer. A guy in front of me at the bar ordered double screwdrivers, and since I love orange juice, that's what I ordered, too. The drinks were ice cold, the air conditioning was on, music was playing, and I had five double screwdrivers in twenty minutes. All I remember after that was falling down and vomiting. Welcome to Vietnam.

"I was in Charlie Company, 1st Cavalry Division, called Airmobile, but oh man, we did a lot of walking! First Cav was a blessing, because Air Cavalry had 435 helicopters. Having a helicopter was like having a horse. I'm alive today because I was with 1st Cav rather than another division. 1st Cav got instant resupply, and most nights we had a hot meal or semi-hot meal. It had been cooked, anyway. They would bring us ammunition, five-gallon jugs of water, mail, and re-stock supplies for the medics. Other units, 4th Infantry or Marines, had to carry it all on their backs.

"At An Khê I found an item I claimed as my good luck charm, something I picked up off a floor. It had what appeared to be praying hands on one side, and an impressive — poem? — on the other side. I secured it around my neck and wore it every hour of every day that I was in Vietnam. Even though I wore it every day, I never could memorize that short saying that was the inscription. When I went home on leave, I would remove and store it away, donning it again when I returned from the latest 25-day drunk.

"The entirety of my first tour of duty over there, I was just an animal. I walked point all the time, which in theory is the most dangerous position. I just didn't give a damn. I knew no fear and would run toward the sound of battle. Make no mistake, I was not one, but I had the honor to walk with lions. I walked with men who had been through one helluva lot before I got to Vietnam. My unit had been in knockdown, dragged out, balls-to-the-wall fighting combat, but I didn't have to do that. We had some hellish battles to start with, then the bad guys left us alone, because we had mobility and firepower.

"For us, there really weren't any rules or regulations. You could just be rootless, and there was freedom to that. It was like camp, like being in Boy Scouts but more organized and better equipped. Beer was cheap or free, cigarettes were free (four packs a day), you didn't have to wear underwear, you didn't have to shave, you didn't have to salute. Throw the cap away when you got a fifth or quart of vodka or whiskey.

"I started a diary in Vietnam, printing everything. Cursive penmanship was a near impossibility on small diary pages soaked with sweat or rain from monsoons. There was no writing surface and often only moonlight to write by. I tried to transcribe my diary when I got out, but the fluids of war made it an impossible task.

"The first combat action I was in happened when I'd been with out in the field maybe 72 hours. We were up on LZ (Landing Zone) Geronimo at the north end of the Bong Son Plains in the hills. This landing zone had bunkers, and about midnight there was a report 'Get your shit on, you're leaving'. Shortly after, our two tanks started moving down off the LZ and out onto the Bong Son Plains to a village. We followed.

"That morning while we were sitting with my squad leader, Larry, who was from Alabama. We heard all these bees buzzing by our heads, flying so fast it was almost like they were breaking the sound barrier. I said, 'Larry, these are some strange sounding bees.' In a southern drawl he replied 'Sam, you dumb son of a bitch. Them ain't bees, them's bullets.'

"Helicopters came and picked us up that

night, and we did the rarest of all things, which is a nighttime air assault. They call them 'air assaults,' but nine times out of ten there wasn't a bullet fired.

"We encircled the village, and the second and fourth platoons went in. There was a hell of a fire fight. There was all kinds of shooting and the tanks also went in. They got shot up pretty damn good so they pulled back.

"That afternoon, my platoon and the 3rd Platoon went in. We were way over on the left-hand flank. You have a platoon of four squads and two fire teams per squad. I'm a Spec 4 (Specialist Fourth Class) so I've got a fire team, and we're moving into the village. I was walking point. Instead of going on the trail, we start going across. We're advancing our line and my fire team is way on the left-hand side, and a Pfc (Private First Class) came running over to me and says, 'There's a couple wounded gooks over here in the ditch.' I did not want him to tell anybody else because I wanted to be the first guy down there to kill those guys. I ran right by my squad leader, went over to the sergeant and said, 'There's two wounded gooks in the ditch. Can I shoot them?' I don't know what he said, but I took it as an affirmative.

"I sprinted back down into this ditch that was about five feet deep. It was an irrigation channel during the monsoon. There's two Vietnamese there, and one of them was wounded. I don't know if the second one was wounded, but they were pulled into the foliage, leaning against the side of the ditch pretending they were dead. As I approached them, the guy in back pushed the guy in front forward and threw an American grenade at me. It landed four feet away from me and it did not explode. American grenades always explode... this one didn't.

"By this time, my sergeant had come up behind me saying, 'Shoot him damn it, shoot him!' and I'm starting to fall back.

"You've got a pistol grip on an M-16, so I

started firing with my right hand, rifle extended, and I shot and killed him. Even with the
rounds fired, that American grenade still did
not explode.

"When you are pulling a trigger you don't
think. It's a helluva experience, but you don't
have words for it. You just have the experience.

"Just like the first time I had sex. I wasn't
thinking about love or responsibility, or mo-
rality or decency; the experience overwhelms
you. It commands your senses, and even if
you talk about it afterwards, you may have se-
quences wrong. The exact same thing happens
when you're pulling a trigger as in the intensi-
ty of sex, crime, death, being arrested by a cop,
or being embarrassed in front of class. I'm just
in the moment."

TWO

The Luck Was Real

Nineteen times over those 18 months he served, Sam survived incidents where he should have been killed or wounded. Death or dismemberment was present for the men around him, but it was never him. What were the odds of that? Sam marveled at it then, and he came to reconcile it in later years when he eventually achieved a deeper understanding of his purpose.

When I asked Sam about the medals winking on his tired old cap, I learned they were not badges for valor to him. They weren't when he received them, and they're certainly not now that he has matured, that he has a more spiritual perspective.

The first near-oblivion experience for Sam happened when his unit was walking through hedgerow country, and the leader called for a break.

"I was in the habit of going 10 feet further before I took off my gear and sat down to have a cigarette," Sam said. "Because it took 15 seconds to walk that bit further, when it was time to leave, by the time the guys behind me get their gear on, it gave me a couple extra minutes. I was going to go on the other side of the hedgerow, because it was shady over there, and I took off my gear, laid it down and walked across the opening to the hedgerow, was standing there taking a leak. I looked down, and there two feet from me was a wire across the opening attached to a buried mortar round. It was a booby trap that would have blown me to kingdom come.

"The luck happened again a day or two before the Tet Offensive, when we air-assaulted a village," Sam recalls. "A heavy weapons unit — I assume it was, because they had rockets — was headed for Da Nang, and we intercepted them. We were dropped outside the perimeter, and firing was heavy. I jumped out of the helicopter, flipped over on my back, and pulled the quick release straps on my pack. Right then, and right where I had been standing, a rocket went in one door and out the other door of the helicopter I just jumped out of. That door gunner must have filled his pants as he saw it coming his way, because there was nowhere to run and nowhere to hide.

"Four minutes later, we were ordered to cross an open dry rice paddy area, probably somewhere between 75 and 100 yards, while the bad guys were in the village shooting at us. Our platoon ran over, and we got there unscathed.

"Most of the roadways there are elevated

because of the monsoons," Sam explains. "We were strung out along the top of the road — Tyson, Evans, Youngdahl, and me, and the next thing I know, I'm lying on my back 15 feet away. I sit up, shake my head, and Youngdahl is laying there flopping and hollering and screaming. I ran over to him, and he was bleeding here and there, but he wasn't spurting, so I left him and ran up to Tyson and Evans, who were laying on top of the road in the fetal position with their hands on their faces. As I got to them, their hands fell away, and they had been decapitated. A B-40 rocket had landed, I'm going to guesstimate six to 12 inches in front of them, and the concussion and the shrapnel that went up killed them both.

"O'Neill was between us writhing on the ground. He'd got some, and then a concussion blew him that way and me this way. I went back to O'Neill and stripped off his gear, stripped off my gear, threw him over my shoulder and, sweet Jesus, it was 100 yards of open rice paddies to carry him. I went up the embankment and ran with him over my shoulder to where the helicopters were coming in. I dropped him off, and said to myself 'now I've got to go back'. I was in the open, without my gear and you just feel naked. I looked down, and here was another grenade laying there. It was one of ours that somebody dropped. I picked the damn thing up and ran back over to where my unit was, holding onto the grenade like you hold onto a lucky rabbit's foot. It was foolish, but I wanted to feel armed. There's a certain comfort to having some kind of weapon in your hand. The one brave thing I did the entire time I was in Vietnam was not done with thought. Delivering O'Neill was pure instinct.

Sam considers this stage of his service time "idiocy or a sense of charmed existence. I just wasn't in touch with fear," he remembers. "There were some people who were trembling, and I wasn't… until the day my point man was killed." He recounts that moment, the day he realized his luck was real but his self-confidence was gone forever.

"I had spent about a month in the rear as a supply sergeant, when we got a new infantry captain. This guy was an incompetent officer, and he ordered everybody in the rear to go back out to the field, including our fat first sergeant. The captain left one supply rep and the company clerk and some malingerers back in the rear.

"An infantry unit is broken into three to five platoons," Sam explains. "I was so damned mad because I'd always been in 1st Platoon. Now I was in 2nd Platoon and I didn't like that. It's just different, maybe it's luck or identification with the unit or whatever.

"Youngdahl was one of the FNGs (F....ing New Guys) sent out to the field the week before. That captain put my squad on point, so I told Youngdahl, 'you go on point.' We're going down the trail, he's tiptoeing from tree to tree and bush to bush, looking for overturned rocks. Everybody's bitchin' because it's hotter than hell, and the packs are heavy. When we took a cigarette break, I told him 'I'm going to walk point and show you how to do it. You sling your rifle, keep your thumb on the selector switch as you go from off to single shot to automatic. You're alert, look at your surroundings, and just follow the trail.' I walked point for him for an hour, until we took another cigarette break. Afterwards I put him back on point. Five minutes later, 'Bang!' One shot through the heart, and he's dead. First guy in line was going to get it. Right then, I knew fear for the very first time.

"At home, you can feel big with your buddies driving down Main Street until the tough guys come, and then you shrink a bit. But in Vietnam I carried my load. In the field you get a reputation, not as bad man, but that you are equal. That felt really good. I thought I'd found a place where I was comfortable, and that was in the field.

"When Youngdahl died, everything was gone. All I knew after that, all I could think about was fear of death."

Sam paused, as if he were pondering whether to go out for another cigarette, then appeared to decide against it. He coughed and shifted his weight in the kitchen chair. Neither of us wanted to stop now, Sam in the telling role and me in the listening role.

"The mantra was you attack an attack. But we did not. There was shooting going on, but we were all remaining prone. I called for the machine gunner, my friend TJ. He was 'short' — about ready to go home. He came running up, dropped down and reached over to his assistant gunner for a belt of ammunition. As the assistant gunner was handing it to him, TJ got shot through the shoulder. As God is my witness, he levitated up off the ground, did a 180 in mid-air and flopped down in front of me, nose to nose. Words have not been invented that I could use to describe what I saw in his eyes.

"He jumped up and started running away. I flipped over on my back and was going to shoot him — 'son of a bitch is abandoning me,' I thought, and I have never done well with that word, mentally, emotionally or physically. I was so tired of being deserted in my life that I was going to kill him. I don't know what stopped me. He wasn't cowardly, he was horrified. He was short, he was so close to getting out.

"After we got ambushed and TJ got shot, we were in a place where we couldn't be evacuated. We had been the first ones in, so now we're the last ones out.

"It was heavy jungle, and we were retreating down a trail that went between two trees, so I took TJ's pack and one from another wounded guy and made a little parapet between the trees. I set up the machine gun there, and guys set claymores (mines that spray steel pellets) and trip flares (cylinders with a fuse, burning stuff inside and a striker, that when the wire is pulled, the striker ignites and illuminates the area). Then we tried to sleep.

"That night one of the guys came over to me, 'Sarge, Sarge! There's somebody over there.' I sat up and listened. I didn't hear anything, so I told him to go back to his position.

"About five minutes later, he came back 'Sergeant, Sergeant! There's somebody out there.' Now I'm pissed off because I'm trying to sleep. So I get up on my knees in my little parapet and listened… flap!… a stick hits me in the forehead."

Sam explains that the Vietnamese threw sticks and stones into American soldiers' positions hoping they would make a noise or pop off a round, giving away their position.

"That's how they mark you. It's as black as the inside of a cow's stomach, you can't see your hand in front of your face, so they throw sticks and that's how they identify where you're at.

"The next morning, the guys on the line reported our tripwire handles had been wrapped, and our claymores had been turned around on us. If we had moved toward whoever was out there in the dark, we would have blown ourselves up. They were pretty damn close. It was an exceptionally small area, which speaks to the dedication and skill of those enemy soldiers. For the first time, I began to think... maybe the competition is better than I am.

"I spent 18 months out in the bush, and I don't remember having the opportunity to fire my M-16 in a combat situation more than 10 times. When I thought about why the hell would that be, it dawned on me that it's all about tactics. If you've got the gun, and I've got the knife, I don't attack you; however, I'll do booby traps or something else. If you've got the mobility and the firepower and the reinforcements and more ammunition, and I'm just 25 people, I'm going to leave you alone and go find a smaller unit I can pick on. So the North Vietnamese basically left us alone when we moved into an area, because of our mobility, instant resupply, and instant reinforcement.

"Weeks later, loaded out of an airport near Saigon, we were on a C-130 flying to a Green Beret base near the Cambodian border to run patrols and provide security when we lost an engine. The crewman said, 'Don't worry.' Then a second engine went out and the crewman said, 'Not to worry, we can fly on two.' We turned around and counted the minutes that seemed like hours until we returned to the safety of Biên Hòa.

Vietnam has three climate zones, Sam explained: the delta with water, the mountainous inland, and the coast. The enemy own the terrain, and to find them you must patrol and let them pick time and place.

"It was mind-numbing, soul-sapping heat and humidity. You move up and down the hills when you are fully loaded, always wet, sweat running off, heaving, gasping, panting from running to the sound of firing, carrying a pack and the platoon radio to the edge of a hamlet. In order to stay hydrated, I carried as much as two gallons of water. Water was always key."

The water was not always good or even safe, but the men got it where they could, when they could.

"Months later, in the mountainous jungle of North Vietnam, we were ambushed," he continued. "We beat a hasty retreat, and being out of water, I drank the best water I've ever had from a mud puddle about five feet across and two inches deep with leaves and bugs. Indelicate sucking was the most effective means of slaking your thirst. Damn, it was good. We filled our canteens and dropped an iodine tablet in each and we drank. Then, 10 minutes later and a hundred yards upstream, there was the massive carcass of a dead water buffalo in the middle of the stream with the water flowing through it."

What the hardship, heat and horrors did to Sam and his comrades for the most part was motivate them to want to get out of Vietnam and soon.

"I was young and strong then", he recalls, "but you never got rested, you wore out, your shoulders and back screamed with aches. We weren't professional soldiers; we thought we were, but we weren't. The Vietnamese have been at war for centuries. First they fought each other, then they fought the French, the Japanese, and then the French and the Dutch. They were pros, we were not.

"At some point after a fire fight, one with all the deadly adjectives you can imagine, there came a time when, like a pack of sled dogs after a long run, we just sat. That thousand-yard stare was real for us — words have yet to be coined that properly limn what the soul and the psyche experienced. Although I had been eager to get into the service, those experiences had changed my mind.

"I had calculated my service time so if I extended my tour of duty twice, I'd come back with less than 180 days to serve, and I'd be out of the damn Army. I wanted out early."

Sam re-upped strategically because there were things during his time there that he valued, emotions that he had never previously enjoyed. He would also never have them again.

"I signed up again, and it wasn't out of patriotism, it wasn't out of intelligence, it was more instinctive. I belonged. This is where I feel good, this is where I'm going to be with brothers in arms. Another part of it was because I wanted my name in the hometown paper. I had written some letters home that my mom shared with the local newspaper publisher, so I'd get letters from people back home.

"When I came home on leave people were glad to see me, and for the first damn time in my life since Debbie, my first girlfriend, it felt like I mattered to another human being in that town. People would tell me 'We're so proud of you' and stuff like that, so I'd smile and say the right thing. If you've never had it before, it's like a dog who's been beaten finally getting used to somebody scratching his ear and petting him.

"All the while I was in Vietnam, my current girlfriend Patsy wrote to me faithfully. I expected letters, never mind that she had her studies and family and was working in a hospital. It was all about me getting mail.

"I was injured just once. We were coming down off this mountain, and I'm going to walk point downhill on a slick, muddy, narrow trail in the jungle. We came around a bend, and here's this North Vietnamese courier swelling up, dead. There's a satchel on his side, and in the satchel was a potato stick grenade, and he had his little finger in the loop of the detonator. You don't know if a bump or a sneeze is going to set it off. We had to step over him, and you're scared to death of slipping and splat, let alone boom!

"We got over him, and the trail down the mountain ravine had been studded with punji sticks (bamboo stakes) as sharp as needles. The enemy would be hiding on the downhill side of that V in the trail and attack. Your instinct is to run uphill, and if you did, you'd be pronged by all the punji sticks.

"As I'm walking down this trail, I stop, and the ground crumbles in front of me: there was a punji pit with stakes about three feet high that would have penetrated my boots all the way to my knees. I'm squatting down, moving the spears aside for us to come through, and I put my hand to push myself up and got one stuck in my arm. I pulled it out, and I'm irrigating it, because they dip the spikes in feces, which is horribly toxic.

"The guy right behind me called for a medic. I started saying, 'I don't need no god d....' and that's as far as I got. My feet slipped, and I went backward and got one in the elbow, right in the crazy bone. I stood up and pulled it out. It was thick jungle, so I had to walk back up to the top of the hill where the Medevac picked me up and took me to the surgical hospital. They took away my Bowie knife, my throwing knife, my grenades, my rifle and my pistol, all this stuff that made me feel secure. While I'm lying there, they carry a guy in on his stomach who had sat on a punji stick, so the whole butt cheek was going to get laid open. Another guy came walking in with the biggest smile on his face — they must have stuck him with a quart of morphine. The outhouses over there were plywood buildings with 55-gallon barrels underneath, and they plumb them out and pour in diesel. He was on the shit burning detail, and when you do that you wear engineer gloves and a sleeveless shirt. From his shoulders to forearms, the true color of every human being was exposed — pink, all of his skin was gone on both arms.

"They lay me on a cot on two saw horses, and a corpsman comes by and takes my shirt off and shaves my armpit. He's got a needle, it was like driving a train engine into my armpit. I could hear it pop. I got to watch them operate. It didn't take long, and they put wire stitches in it.

"Those were some of the 19 times I had luck. I didn't realize it at the time, but there had to be a god involved, because of the number of should have, could have, would have, ought-to-die times. It is just beyond the odds of comprehension that I was still alive and unscathed. Looking back now I know there was something else going on, but at the time I was lost and such a wretched wannabe. I would not know that for 30 more years.

"Late one afternoon, a few of us were sitting around before we settled into positions on the perimeter of our encampment for the night. Our squad leader, Larry, a stereotypical southern white, tall, lean, lanky with a casual drawl, and Mel, a shorter, slender, and wiry black, were from the same town in Alabama. These two had been through combat hell prior to my joining the unit. You swap stories, share smokes and lights, tales of home and youthful adventures, worries, hopes, desires and dreams. You become as intimate as males in their late teens and early twenties can be. Then Larry made a comment I have never forgotten: 'It ain't gonna be like this when we get home, is it.' It was not a question.

"People had what we called DROST (date of return to the states), and there was a continual rollover. It felt uncomfortable that guys I served with were going home, guys that you cared about and you felt like they cared about you. Yeah, we'll stay in touch, we said, and so forth. After my own DROST, what was I going to do then?

"I fancied myself a store manager, a retailer. I'm great at unloading trucks and putting stuff on the shelf or carrying it out the front door. Didn't know crap about developing relationships with brokers, insurance agents, bankers, and those are the essence of a business. Someday I'm going to college, and I'm going to do this or I'm going to do that, but the reality is you're sitting there scratching yourself and eating out of a can. I had thoughts, but none of it was wisely calculated in terms of a vision of life. It was about getting out, going home and drinking beer, and getting married.

"When I left Vietnam in June 1969, I'd had hepatitis from a cheeseburger in Sin City outside An Khê, and the punji stick injury, but otherwise I was untouched. I saw people injured or killed in all kinds of ways, and my suffering was nothing. When people say 'Oh, poor Sam was in Vietnam,' I keep my mouth shut, because I know the truth: I didn't have it bad at all. It was an adventure. There was more trauma with the breakup with my first girlfriend than there was in anything over there.

"Yet inside me there was nothing. I felt like an empty rubber beach ball bouncing through the air. It doesn't make any difference whether it's salt water or fresh water, sun or darkness, sand or dirt. Just this ball rolling through life, and nothing is absorbed. Nothing. Later on maybe a grain of sand gets in the seam, and eventually it ruptures, but there was just nothing inside. And if there was God anywhere, for me at that time, it was mostly goddamn sons of bitches out there."

Aloneness Embedded

That empty beach ball feeling was born long before he was in Vietnam.

In our coffee-fueled mornings at his kitchen table or sitting in his office, Sam spoke with level calm and without blame about his parents. His father, who owned and ran a store, and his mother, a former R.N., adopted him and a younger sister — each from different mothers — through a Catholic organization. They were ordinary small midwestern town people trying to live the post-World War II dream of peace, a family, stability and modest abundance.

On the outside, they were respectable, average folks. On the inside, it turned out, they did irreparable damage to their son.

"How I became who and what I was in Vietnam and after the service, was not due to, at any early age, beating, rape, starvation, drugs, alcohol, etc., nor living in a distinct environment," he explains. "No ghetto, no physical impairment or disfiguring, no persistent, methodical diminishment by those around me.

"Vietnam gave me a sense of camaraderie I had never had before — or at least a taste of it. The unit gave a sense of place and purpose, right or wrong. If I was the second guy in the foxhole and could do my bit and stay awake, or if I could carry the load in the field, and there are just 85 or 125 of us, and that's all we got, I was part of something. You really felt like you mattered. To people who say PTSD from Vietnam caused me to do what I did over the next several years, I say 'bullshit.' I started having

PTSD when I was six."

We break for a quick stretch, in my case, and a smoke for Sam. While he's on the deck, I scrutinize the photographs on the wall of his living room. The classic 1950s black and white photos show Sam's father, lean in a short-sleeved white shirt, his face grim, unsmiling and watchful behind equally plain glasses, gives nothing away. His mother wears a shirt-waist summer dress and her classic brunette pageboy is styled in Wave-Set curls. Sam with a blonde crew cut and wide striped t-shirt holds his baby sister.

There are later photos of Sam himself in military uniform: dark eyebrows and hair, sleepy eyelids, full lips in just a suggestion of a smile, a handsome, almost Boy Scout-ish young man.

"Mom was a smiler, friendly with the staff at the hospital, the doctors and the pharma-cists, and she had a bag full of pill bottles," Sam continued. "She was horribly overweight and had no self-esteem, and years later Dad told me she was also into the booze. I do not ever recall one word of father-son or mother-son from them. Nothing, absolutely nothing. There was no connection. We were four people living in the same house, that's all."

When asked what he remembers about his earliest life, Sam pauses, then speaks thoughtfully, as the images rise in his imagination.

"What do I recall? In our first home, we lived on the edge of a small prairie farm town on a gravel road. Dad had a little bit of sand dumped there for a sand box for us to play in. I had no trucks or cars or anything like that, but Mom and Dad had just given me a Roy Rogers six gun and holster set for my fifth or sixth birthday. So I was out there one day, wearing my Roy Rogers set, and this big kid, probably eight or nine, came walking down the road, and he had a little green army Jeep. We talked for a minute or two, and he said, 'Let's trade.' So I traded my gun and holster set for that Jeep, because I had no trucks or cars. He strapped on the gun and holster set, then he reached out and took that Jeep and threw it in a field of weeds so far that it would be impossible for me to ever find and he took off down the road. When my dad came home, his message to me was 'How could you be so stupid? What's wrong with you?'

"At that moment, the door started to slam in me, and I pulled back into myself."

That he was completely alone crushed his heart. Sam had no friends to bolster him. His younger sister, little more than a toddler, was no consolation. Innocent and trusting, he'd been duped, then shamed. There was no one on his side, a harsh blow that was to be followed by more throughout the years of his childhood.

"After that, a series of other events shaped me," Sam told me. Later he was to say these events "misshaped" him and I learned that was tragically true. He was an adopted child, a choice of sorts made by his parents, but he was not a wanted child, a valued or protected child. His worst memories illustrate that repeatedly.

"One winter day, Mom was pissed at me about something, and she smacked a quarter in my hand, put a coat on me and pushed me out the back door, and said, 'Get!' Did she want me to leave—forever? Where was I to go?

"When I was about seven, it was a hot summer day, some friends came to visit my parents, and I was sent out to their car to fetch something. A couple hours later, they went to drive home and couldn't get into their car; the keys were locked inside. Dad came out, and I got the blame. It didn't matter whether I did it or not. Again his message to me was 'How could you be so stupid? What's wrong with you? Don't you know any better?'"

Sam's psyche was being formed by those he depended on, and the closed identity that was taking shape in the small boy would take him years to identify and repair as a man.

"It wasn't just the criticism," he told me. "There was a void where there should have been kindness, forgiveness, explanations or help. There was no guidance, just consequences."

This distance from love, kindness and intimate gentleness would magnify throughout his life.

"They never asked me how school was going, never cuddled me, never read stories or sang to me. Never, at least not in my memory. It just didn't happen. By age six or seven, I was locked in, or I was heading that way. My aloneness was real and embedded."

"What word would you use to describe how you felt throughout your life at home?" I asked him.

"Aloooooooone," he answered, drawing it out in his baritone voice. "And inside I was just crying, 'please, somebody notice me, somebody love me.'"

Beaten down in spirit by his parents, Sam suffered consequences from other children as well.

"When I was 10, we moved to a pretty neat and tidy little town. We lived in a nice three-bedroom house in a new area, a bit of small town suburbia. The third or fourth day I was there, I ventured out of the house to go downtown, and as I walked past a house, a guy came out of the door. He'd never seen me before in his life, but he beat me up. He did it one more time, too, later on. You see, I was not raised to be combative or anything like it, I was raised to be submissive."

For many kids, pets are a loving refuge. Even if parents are distant or abusive, a dog or cat provides love and certain comfort.

"We had a Weimaraner and he had free run of the town and house, but he was not something that you cuddled with. We also had Tom the cat, and he was pretty damn independent as well. My dad got me raising rabbits, but they were not pets.

"My Halloween candy was stolen, and my

dog ran away, and each time Dad was too busy to give a damn. He knew the dog would come back, but I didn't. Each time the message from him was, 'You're on your own.' So I didn't tell my parents anything, because the message was clear: don't do anything in word or deed to ever discomfort anyone. We don't care if it's right or wrong, shut up and swallow it. We've got no time for you, and we've got no time for this.'

"My escapes were reading and movies. As a store owner, Dad and every other business-man in town had to buy a magazine subscrip-tion from every kid and adult selling them. I devoured every page, read countless books, watched TV, and paid attention to the news.

"Dad started me bagging stock for 10 cents for every 100 pounds at his store. I discovered money with which I paid my own way and saw *South Pacific* and *Bridge on the River Kwai* in a big, plush old theater like they used to make them. The movie theater was only three blocks down Main Street from our house. Going to a movie at night with huge old elm trees towering over the road, especially in the moonlight, scared me to death, but I would go anyway. Even today, I could walk there to the seat I used to sit in all the time. Me, a movie and a box of my favorite candy, Boston Baked Beans.

"Mom helped Dad part time at the store, where she had this smarmy way of 'It's so good to see you.' There was none of that attentive kindness at home. At home she had the aches, pains, grunts and the groans. If somebody was coming over, there would be a flurry of activity. We had to get cardboard boxes and put all the dirty laundry in it — she didn't have the energy to do it — and then take it to the dump. She had surgery once or twice, but that was always hush-hush, too. You don't ever talk about it. Everything was 'shut up,' 'shut up,' 'shut up.'

"There may have been a cursory something or another at the table, such as 'Sam, I need you to come to work in the morning.' Otherwise there was zero, and I mean zero, communication in my family. We spoke at one another, we were not raised to speak with one another. There was never a question of 'how was your day?' or 'what's new with you?' or what have you. I don't think my parents were that way with each other, either.

"I don't know if Mom and Dad ever had a conversation about anything other than what TV channel to put on or what's for supper; both of them just endured. It was a very non-communal way of having a family. I had food, shelter and clothing, but nothing of substance instilled by communication with my parents. I guess if there is one word to describe who and what I was to them it would be 'Wrong.' I knew I was not good enough. I do not remember a single word of 'Attaboy!'

"A couple of summers, I stayed with an uncle, aunt, and my cousins. My sister didn't go along, and I suspect my parents wanted just me to be away. My uncle and cousins and I would play golf, we did some bike riding, and I saw some positive stuff. I had a feeling there was more of a relationship between them than between me and Dad. Something was missing. It was groin deep and real, and I didn't recognize or attempt to find what was gonna take to make me whole."

What kind of man does a boy become, when his parents scorch his soul with emotional indifference, neglect and outright hostility, I wondered? Over the early visits of sitting with Sam, listening, occasionally both of us blowing our noses and wiping tears away, I was going to learn those consequences to him and to others.

"Mom was a schmoozer so she was always tight with the parish priest and the Ladies' Aid. We had it all going at the Catholic church, where I was an altar boy in training with Father Michael, a stereotypical little Irish priest with a brogue and white hair. He seemed to me like a wonderful guy. In this cute little town, the kids had all been raised together, and I went to school with Lutherans of different ilks, Presbyterians, Methodists, two or three different kinds of Dutch Reform. Every church was 'The one,' maybe clearest of all our Catholic church. One day we're sitting there at the rectory, and one of the other guys asked Father Michael something about a particular person who was not a Catholic. I thought Father was going to cry. He said, 'I'm sorry, but he won't be able to go to heaven.' I was mildly shocked and filed that away.

"When I was in tenth grade, on a pretty cold winter day, I didn't have any gloves. A friend of my sister had left some at our house, so I was going to wear them and bring them back after school. My sister started screaming 'Don't take them!' I said, 'I'll bring them back' and started heading towards the back door. Out of nowhere, my mother appeared and started beating me, beating me, beating me. I managed to get the door between us and rushed off to school. Not five minutes after I arrived, over the PA system I heard 'Sam, report to the principal's office!' Dad was there and took me out of school. As we drove home, I told him what happened, but he took Mom's side. I got spanked. I didn't deserve it and Dad knew it, But Mom wanted it, so Dad spanked me.

"Whatever we had was over with. It was done…they just became two more human beings in my life. I had been betrayed by each of them in small ways, and this was the curtain drawn between us. There was nothing that either one of them could do or say that would lead me to trust them again. I was on that path anyway, but this time it felt so damn distinct. It told me a lot about who my dad really was — one fearful man.

"He was raised during the Depression, he experienced being a serviceman during World War II, and his store was how he identified himself. It was his sanctuary, that store, and he wanted to protect it, because that was his refuge from me, from the world, from life. I loved working there, too, putting things on the shelves and carrying stuff out the door. I knew where every item in the store was shelved, the price, how many the shelf held, its width and depth. I liked what I did, and that was also a safe place for me. I knew how to work like hell in the store, and that also meant money: $4.00 in your pocket may not be much today, but that was a lot to a teenager in the 1960s. It was a point of pride for me that I bought presents for Mom and Dad, my sister and other people. I was particular about what I bought, thoughtful about it."

Sam's small efforts to find family, to create a place where he could belong or feel welcome, included athletics as well as school.

"I would try sports, but I just never felt a part of anything. In football, the few times the coach put me in, I'd knock somebody on their butt, but I didn't know how to live the other 99% of the time, and other people did.

They seemed more popular with the coaches and more successful. I don't know what they received, all I know is what I did not. So I didn't have any friends to speak of. I was a little world unto myself, looking for that path of least resistance.

"English and geography were not a problem, and history was my easiest, best subject. The math teacher, God bless him, he D+ me or D- me through, because I didn't know a damn thing, and I would not ask for help; it was much the path of least resistance. Math was a disaster and so were biology and any other sciences. They fascinated me, but I am not a studier, and for those subjects you're talking study and learning, whereas literature was easy. Literature I could just absorb.

"A good memory is what got me the lead in 'Our Town' in junior year of high school. I wanted to be famous, and because I associated with a lot of people in Dad's business, I was not shy about dealing with people. When I tried theatre it was all about me and my ego. It was about accolades I thought I was going to get for my performance."

Sam felt competent and safe at his father's store, the only place where he could peacefully put things into a structure. Away from his volcanic mother, the school and neighborhood bullies, he toiled in the back room unloading goods, creating order and neatness on shelves, taking inventory.

"Throughout school, I worked at the store weekends and after school hours, and although Dad paid me less than everybody else, I also didn't have regulated hours. I felt special that I had money, and I bought myself things; I'd see a picture of a model airplane or a ship, and I would buy the kit. I'd start fiddling with it, and instead of taking two or three weeks I'd end up slapping it together and painting it and putting on decals while the glue was still wet. That was a good metaphor for the rest of my life. Even if someone had been there to help me, I would not have followed instructions. I was guideless, but in my world, in the early to mid '60s, you didn't need a guide. The message I got was you're a white male in America, and we've just saved the world from the evils of everything. We can do it all. You should do it all, and if you need help, there's something wrong with you."

Throughout his childhood and well into high school Sam lived with that deep sense of being faulty and a disappointment. He retreated from any expectation of love from anyone. His was not just typical teen alienation, it was something more, and it was to have consequences. Then, briefly, there was a girl.

"I lived for years before I believed somebody cared," he said "That person was Debbie. I was 17 and she was, I think, 15. She was the instigator, the first girl I had sex with. And boy, this was love forever! I was ready to drop out of high school, get a job and get married and live happily ever after. It was *Leave it to Beaver* and *All in The Family* and *Father Knows Best* all in one.

"Ten months later, she dumped me. Mom and Dad, for some reason, were gone right then and left me alone at home for three days. I didn't go to school. Loneliness is pain, and you can only absorb so much before you start putting it on to other people, and then you really don't give a damn, you don't know how to. I felt that loneliness.

"By spring 1966, when I got out of high school, I had no conscience, and that had enabled me to live. I was this little ball of disaster looking for a place to explode. Along about June it came to me, my dad don't want me here. I had the idea I would work at the store, but he had a guy working for him who was a year or two older than me, and he'd go to him rather than me for conversation. I got the sense that Dad expected me to do something else, and I didn't know what. His only words of advice to me were, 'Work for the government or be a doctor,' and I understood that was clearly not an invitation to be in business with him.

"About July, I realized he expected me to go to college, but I should have been applying six months earlier, so what am I going to do? I always liked ships, and I had read *Horatio Hornblower* and all this naval stuff, so I ran over and joined the Navy, signed for four years on a four-month delayed entry program. I did it with zero consultation with any other human being. That felt good for a few weeks. Then by August I got thinking, four years is a long time, so I tried to volunteer for the local draft — that's three years rather than four. They'd already made their selections through February, so I went to a town in a nearby state and told the Army recruiter I wanted to join. I said to him, 'There's one problem — I've already joined the Navy.' He said, 'No problem, we can arrange that,' and I signed up for three rather than four years of service. I didn't know anything about the military specialties then or that I could be a cook or a military policeman or a clerk typist, so I volunteered for infantry airborne, not because I was full of guts and glory, but because I really wanted them to take me.

"The most miserable damn three days of my life to that point (and probably his, too) were when Dad decided he needed to take me fishing before I went over to Vietnam. I can think of a zillion things I'd rather have done than go up north with him. There was nothing of substance between us, and you can try and manufacture it and conjure up something, but there wasn't. The most feeling I had for him, where it comes to anything, was years later when my mom died, then I knew he cared for her, but my dad and I were forever distant.

"The Saturday before I left for the service, my buddy Jack and I were driving to a café in a larger town, and there was a car parked alongside the road. We slowed down to see if they had some car problem, and Jack looked over into the car and then said, 'Get the hell out of here!' or something to that effect — it was two guys kissing!

"We got to the café, where a girl named Patsy and some of her friends came walking in, and they were talking about it, so we'd seen it and they'd seen it. Patsy was a senior in high school, just a year behind me, and after we talked, I found out her last name and where she lived and gave her a ride home.

"The next day we're having a family gathering, and I'm going in the army on Monday morning, so I told Mom that I had met a girl — could I invite her? She said sure, so I pulled open the phonebook and called Patsy up, and she came over.

"Monday morning, I had my little bag in hand, and I signed the papers and raised my hand and took the oath, got on the bus to the airport, and landed in Fort Polk, Louisiana. Eight weeks later, I was shipped to Fort Gordon, Georgia for another eight weeks of training. On leave, I saw Patsy every available minute, because there was sex, and I was in love and a man now.

"I was six to eight weeks shy of my 19th birthday and, out of character, one Sunday morning in Georgia I went to the base PX and bought a Sunday paper and a small pitcher of beer. I finished the paper... but not the beer. That would be much different later on, with devastating consequences to others."

FOUR

Can't Give What You Don't Have

In the late Sixties and early Seventies, Sam was a young, strong, handsome returning veteran in an epoch of smashing boundaries, of the pursuit of pleasure, of experimentation. My fellow students and I called a national strike, and marched in our bell bottoms and hiking boots by the thousands carrying signs and brandishing banners against the Vietnam War, against President Nixon and U.S. imperialism. Others famously and photogenically stuck daisies in the muzzles of National Guard rifles or got tear gassed by city cops. We were full of righteous rage, optimism, good music and not always so good drugs, and we ardently believed we could change the world for the better for everyone. In that tumultuous time, Sam's inner emptiness roared head on fueled by a desire for what he decribes was 'satiation in the moment'.

"My parents had no part in our decision when Patsy and I got married that August after I returned from service," he told me. "I tried to seduce her maid of honor the night before the wedding, because I had no sense of decency.

"Being married is not buying a house and having sex, which is how I thought of it when I was 21 and home from Vietnam. It's developing a relationship with another person who's going to be there good, bad, and indifferent. I didn't have any of that, and we can't give what we don't have.

"While I was in Vietnam, Patsy did a year studying medical technology and did well. After the wedding, we moved into a little apartment and both started going to junior college three or four days later. About two days after that, I discovered keg parties, and I discovered women at keg parties.

"A good share of the women I was involved with were the aggressors, which surprised me, because I was raised to think women were sacred and holy. When I held the door for one, I was scared to even touch her hand. This gave me one more thing to question about how I was raised.

"Patsy wasn't against having a beer, and for her, drinking was not addictive, but for me, it was like going to the state fair. I was having fun, I had a new car Dad had bought me, I had money, people were glad to see me, and what more could an irresponsible man want?

"Three or four months later, I'm drinking and driving and partying and raising hell, and I was broke. I went to Dad and said, 'Can I borrow $75 for new tires for the car, because your daughter-in-law is pregnant with your first grandchild, and I need some good tires?' Then I bought an old spare and spent the rest of the money partying and boozing.

"One night that first year back, my friend Jack and his girlfriend, and Patsy and I were drinking beer and eating chitlins at a bar. As we're leaving, boom, there goes Jack running past followed by two bikers. He had decided to steal one of their helmets, which was not a good thing. I got Jack and his girlfriend in the back of the car, and Patsy and I got in front, and one biker cussed us out and said, 'Come on, let's kick in his lights!' Now this is personal, they're talking about me, my car. One was going to kick in the headlights, and the other one was hustling back to jump up on the trunk and kick in the back window. I stomped on the gas. One went flying and the next one went flying, and now the adrenaline is going, and I lost all sense of clarity. These guys are standing between the pumps at the gas station, kicking at my car as I go through, and I'm going out on the avenue and coming back around fast and trying to run them down and kill them. The girls are screaming, and Jack is yelling, 'Get 'em, Sam!' Then I looked kitty-corner across the street, and there was a cop. He was slunk way down behind the steering wheel with his lights off, because he didn't want no part of what was going on. Suddenly something clicked. 'This is enough,' and I decided discretion is the better part of valor here, and we headed for home.

"I submerged my temper, my loneliness, my despair and fear, but it came out sometimes when I found a way to act out like that. Another one of those ways—the usual way — was drinking.

"In May, I went to a kegger at a park on a lake, and the last thing I remember was wading in the lake up to my knees and then volunteering to go get more beer. I woke up in the hospital three days later. Patsy was sitting there and told me what happened. I'd been drunk and speeding, and I rolled the car. One guy in the back seat had a broken leg, the other had a broken arm, and the guy in my passenger seat was killed."

He had felt nothing for the men he killed in Vietnam, and Sam felt equally nothing now for the young partygoers who had been riding in his car. The hometown hero who had enjoyed all the publicity while he was serving in Vietnam was becoming something darker and more self-centered.

"My first thought when I got out of the hospital was how could I get a cigarette. The second thought was when could I get a beer, and the next thought was when am I going to call one of my girlfriends.

"I saw my car, and the roof was substantially lower, the steering wheel was caved in, and the driver's seat was halfway twisted around backwards. How the hell I lived through it, I'll never know, but I was just pissed off because my brand-new Charger had been wrecked, and I was reduced to driving a 1959 brown four-door Ford, a farmer's car.

"Right out of the hospital, I was scheduled to speak at the Memorial Day services. I got drunker than a skunk on the way there, and I'm a mouthy, uneducated, opinionated, ill-formed, emotionally-based, spiritually dead, stupid son of a bitch, and I got up there and made an ass out of myself.

"There was this little volcano going on inside me, and I wanted to be something, but I didn't know how. So it erupted mostly in inopportune ways and at inopportune times. It came out that day at the speech as how great I am and how stupid the rest of you are — it's embarrassing to even think about now.

"Withdrawal was my preferred tactic. I never officially dropped out of junior college, but I walked away from it after the car accident. I wasn't dead but so spiritually diseased and emotionally unwell that I walked away from being a husband and father, too. Our son David was born in 1971, and I never held him except at church on the day he was baptized, I was that far detached.

"I couldn't identify with others, it was all about protecting myself and avoiding pain. I would see stuff on TV, westerns and movies about World War II, and being brothers forever. I wanted that, the band of brothers I thought we had in Vietnam, but we didn't stay in touch. There was no human being on the face of this earth I felt I could trust. So I drank at the American Legion Club, the Eagles, the VFW, small places, the only places where I felt comfortable. I didn't feel good playing softball or golf, but I could sit there and drink and be a wannabe. The bar was sanctuary, it was safety with all the other lost people.

"I mostly drank beer, although I was not shy about mixed drinks or a fifth of whiskey or vodka. I didn't much give a damn, I just wanted alcohol. It varied by circumstances: I drank 'til I ran out of money, sometimes 'til I couldn't drink any more, or I had to be someplace at a certain time.

"And I'd have a nanosecond of remorse or guilt when I saw Patsy, and I was having an affair, because she was a good person, but you will do anything to yourself or anyone else not to experience pain. I encouraged Patsy to leave me, which she did, and the old man fronted me some money, and I moved into a trailer. One day she showed up at his store, and we sat in Dad's office and talked; we got back together for a while, but things never improved."

At Razor's Edge

What does disconnection drive a man to do? Much, and none of it good at this stage of his life, Sam assured me. There's no more powerful drug in the world than if somebody cares, he said, but the reverse of that is the psychosis or the madness of loneliness. He dealt with it in the ways a lost soul would.

"In 1974, I got locked up for a sex offense. It was the stereotypical thing: I was at a dance hall and a woman and I were drinking. She didn't say no; she didn't say yes, either. But afterwards, she told some other guy at the dance hall what a jerk I was and he called the cops.

"They started off with the charge of aggravated rape, and it ended up being indecent liberties, which was a more correct charge. My attorney was a pretty sharp guy, and I probably could have gotten off. The judge had been the district attorney when I was going to college and knew about the drunk driving accident, so he relished the chance to do something with me. I was convicted, and rightly so, even though I denied it.

"During that time, a local counselor gave me copies of the 12 Step recovery program books. I read them from cover to cover, saw some interesting things, then put them away. I went to one meeting and didn't go back. I didn't understand recovery, I thought it was a matter of go to meetings and don't drink. I didn't start going spiritually until I was ready, years later.

"After the trial and before sentencing, I

worked for two or three weeks managing a store. I disapproved of people smoking at the register, and a cashier was doing that, so I told her so. A day or two later, when she went to the restroom, she left her purse by the scale instead of taking it with her. Then she talked with the supervisor, who came to me and said, 'Betty says you took 10 dollars out of her purse.' It was a small town, everyone knew I was out on paper (bail) and heading to prison. The supervisor for sure knew, and I got fired. I never took the 10 dollars. Now nobody in my hometown would have anything to do with me.

"I knew a woman whose husband had gotten me the job, and she and I had necked a bit once or twice, and there was the promise of more. So I'm figuring, well, here's the easiest one available, and I drove to their apartment when her husband wasn't home and knocked. She opened the door, looked at me and said, 'No, we're done.' And I'm kind of on my last legs, because I don't have much to hope for or to feel good about. She started to slam the door in my face, and I hadn't thought about this before, but I reached in my pocket for my box cutter. I was going to kill her. As soon as my fingers touched it — this is the God's truth — as soon as the fingers of my right hand touched my razor, I imploded. I sprinted down the hallway of the apartment building, down the steps, out to my car. The only thing I could think of was getting to the highway. I got going and turned east and sat there holding the steering wheel doing 70 mph. It would be the first time I cried out to God for help.

"I don't know to this day if I was out for two seconds, 20 seconds or two minutes, but I came to, and the first thing I thought was I'm still doing 70 mph. The next thing I realized was the obsession to drink had been removed. Bam! Alcohol was just gone. Since then I never had the obsession to drink, and I feel for other people who still struggle with that. (I do struggle with cigarettes.) I turned the car around and went home, and then I went on a dry drunk for 23 years.

"Right before sentencing for indecent liberties, I had an epiphany moment: I realized that what I had done was wrong, so I wrote a letter to the judge and said so. My attorney told me that was not a wise thing to do, but it felt clean doing that, and besides, I was not noted for consulting anyone about anything."

Sam was sentenced to four years, and first, to avoid a stay at the security hospital for psychoanalysis on his crime, he entered the VA hospital for Gestalt therapy, which was a new fad.

"Gestalt therapy was a way to vent in front of another person and be open about it, but I could do that by bitchin' about the wife while drinking at a bar," he explained. "Under Dr. M. I'm conjuring up I'm-mad-at-my-dad and stuff like that, beating a bat on a mattress, and none of it was real. It's like spray painting over the rust on a car; it doesn't get to the root cause. It was just play acting.

"Then I realized that the more well-fed, the more well-rested, the more satiated I am, the less able I am to be real. So I talked him into doing a marathon group, twenty-four hours, with most of the rest of the men in the unit –- 15 or 20 of us — along with him and a couple of nurses. We did it, and the superficial how-you-doing bullshit starts off, and by about the twelfth hour the real stuff starts coming out. That was insightful, it helped instill in me the value of the façade we live behind that defends us from having to look at who and what we really are. It's not in a psychiatric textbook or easily explained, and it's made worse by the latest guy with 25 years of schooling who's come up with some new model or excuses of how you became who you are.

"Some are valid, I understand that. Well, yeah, bad things and good things happen to most of us in varying degrees. There are psychological reactions to those for many, but when I'm contemplating violence or lust, I don't have time to sit down and start going through 32 pages of text."

SIX

Prison 101 and the Go-To Guy

His desire to drink had been dramatically excised in a way I'd never heard in decades of 12 Step meetings. It was obvious, nonetheless, that despite therapy and that written apology, Sam would find himself behind bars.

That's where he was about to meet a modified, modern and low key form of guardian angel.

"After that Gestalt therapy experience, the deputy sheriffs delivered me to prison," he continued. "Standing outside the wire-topped walls, I was in awe. I'd heard the stories, and it looked grim, imposing and intense. I was befuddled by the sights and sounds, wondering what goes on in there, and not knowing what was waiting behind the door.

"This state penitentiary has a long history of being a tough damn place inside the walls. A guy in protective custody got murdered there, and later I learned from my friend Bruce, another prisoner, how he was standing on the tier one day, and an Indian fellow came walking down the tier holding his intestines — he'd just been cut open. It was not a nice place, although it was better than it had been in the past. Yet, like the luck I had in Vietnam, miraculous things happened to me in that prison. It would take years, but I was on my way, although I didn't know it at the time, toward a kind of grace.

"Like most new arrivals, I was put in the receiving block. At first I was working in the factory line, where they put most of the new guys to keep them busy while they decide where you're going to be assigned. I appeared before the assignment committee, and next thing I know, I'm a clerk in an air-conditioned subsection of the prison. I worked for a lieutenant in an office annex that held the associate warden's secretary, a prison prosecuting officer, the prison DA (district attorney), and his secretary. I typed up cell hall changes and sorted time cards for guards. I was right across the hall from the canteen, close to the ice machine, and that was real convenient.

"The prison had these kiosks with brochures about 'We're going to save your soul' or 'You should get a job' or what have you. I'd only been there a few days when I saw a brochure about Amicus. I thought 'what the hell is this?' I read it, and it didn't have an agenda. It said they're just going to introduce you to somebody, so I filled the application out and sent it in, and a guy by the name of Joe showed up.

"Joe became my Go-To Guy. When the

poop is coming out of my ears, and I'm tired of doing it my way, in times of crisis, I've called Joe. During those times, Joe, my Amicus buddy, stuck with me. He is a straitlaced guy, not dogmatic but a moral person, and so is his wife Joy. At first, he would visit me and we'd sit and talk. Then later, Joe and Joy invited me to their home like they would anybody else; to them it didn't matter that I was Mr. Convict. It was always a nice interlude to go swimming or fishing on their pontoon boat, to do yard work with them, to be invited to be part of something. They made it exceedingly easy. I met their son and daughter and their neighbors.

"Who the hell would want to visit a sex offender and not be subtly snooty about it?" he wondered. "And who would dare to introduce you to his family and invite you to his home? He had a sense I was not going to use him, he wasn't in danger nor was his family. I felt comfortable being with them, and I was exposed to a sense of normalcy, of what life and a family can be.

"It took a while for it to grow on me, to understand who they were. I was aware of the pristine way in which they lived compared to how I lived. Joe was very diligent about everything, as opposed to my slap dash approach toward life. He was doing the next right thing no matter what whether it was taking out the trash or being a 30-year employee of a company or changing oil on the garden tractor. And perhaps most astonishing to me, Joe and Joy treated their kids civilly, maturely, with positive, humane words. I didn't hear fault finding or complaining. That's the way they were raised, and it was what you do.

"When we are kids, we need someone — a parent, usually — to say, 'I've had troubles, too, and here is how you deal with it.' I didn't have that family, but now I was seeing it with Joe's family.

"Amicus was foundational to me, in a subtle way it was part of me rejoining the human race. A lot of time we don't know the significance at the time, but we are formed by that and those around us.

"There were other surprises. I came back from work one day, and my cell house sergeant said 'There's a brand new set of blues in your office. A guy's coming to pick you up tonight. Be at the rotunda at 6:00 p.m.'

"I put on the stuff, the door to the cell hall opened, and we walked down to the rotunda. Here's this civilian who loads me in his car and takes me to a 12 Step meeting. At that meeting, for the first time, I recognized the inscription on what I had carried as my good luck charm in Vietnam — The Serenity Prayer: 'God grant me the serenity to accept the things I cannot change, the courage to change the things I can, and the wisdom to know the difference.'

"One day later on, the warden shows up and says, 'Sunday mornings there's a church meeting — would you be able to talk to the kids?' Well, sure. Next thing I know here's a new pair of jeans and shirt in my cell. The guard lets me out, here's the warden, we drive downtown, stop and have a donut, and then go to the church. Things like that don't normally happen to people in prison, but for me it went on and on. It turns out that the prison DA was my hometown attorney's stepson. Without talking with my father, the attorney called his stepson and said, 'Sam is coming up there. If you can help, would you?' So there was stuff going on behind the scenes all the time, and I didn't see this in the background. It was all about chest-thumping me.

"Of my four-year sentence I spent four months inside the walls and ten months in the minimum security unit. It's a large two-story building with no bars on the windows, two or three guards on duty downstairs in the office area, and upstairs rapists, car thieves, murderers, burglars, a lot of loners, and violent men who had done a huge amount of time inside already.

"Such as we were capable of making, we had a few decent friendships, and it was a sweet place to be rather than inside the prison, which was again lucky, because the other building could be hell. The longer you live there, the more privileges you are eligible for. With Joe as an escort, I could sign out to attend 12 Step meetings or church or make a holiday visit to Mom and Dad.

"Through Joe, another Amicus volunteer called me, and I got asked to serve on the board of Amicus. I was not being the bad man when they asked me, so I agreed to it. I put on a clean suit, got releases and showed up for meetings where I met a county prosecutor, the chief justice of the state supreme court, and various media people. I gave a few talks to Lions Clubs, Rotary Clubs and church groups on what Amicus is. I did some volunteering, visiting a guy in prison named Audie, a mean, angry son of a bitch who will be there the rest of his life.

"It was intimidating to be on the board, as if a bunch of seniors asked a kindergartener to eat lunch with them. I learned a lot, and I was pretty diligent and appreciated the concept of Amicus; that is what drove me. The theory is when you are released, you'll head for the old familiar bar unless you are being introduced to more socialized circumstances and people. Amicus hit upon how people grow up, and it's companionship, daring to associate with people not like you. That's pretty wise: a district court judge came up with the idea of introducing prisoners to adults out there, mature adults without agendas, who could be accepting, no lectures, no preaching, no guidance, but who have an effect just by example. He had faith, hope and trust that people would pick up on it, but it takes a long time.

"During that first time I served in prison, my second child was born. My first son is my son, but Mark, my second one, may not be. I'll never be able to prove this, but I believe Patsy was having an affair with somebody while I was in prison, which is not unheard of.

From minimum security, he applied for admission to the work release program, it was approved, and Sam went to live at the downtown Salvation Army.

"They had a good system going there with all the different resources and books for anything you need to find a job. They would also run off copies and do postage, and I mailed 30 or 40 resumes out with job applications.

"Tom Thumb offered me a job, Orkin offered me a job, and I got one other offer. I ended up taking the job at Tom Thumb, and the first couple of weeks, although I didn't know how to ride the bus, I had to go to one of 52 different stores every day. Transportation was kind of tough. Then they gave me a store to manage, and Joe helped me get an old station wagon so I could drive to my job in the suburbs. Soon Tom Thumb offered me a store managership because they wanted to sell beer there. The corporation couldn't apply for the license, it had to be an individual. I started out 50 or 60 hours a week, opening the place at 6:00 a.m. or quarter to 7:00 a.m., five and six days a week.

"I kept attending 12 Step meetings, and I fell in love with what I perceived of the program. Even though I was not drinking, I didn't follow the whole program. I was young then, and while a lot of young people come to recovery, a lot of them are also not ready to settle down and be spiritual. One day at the meeting, lo and behold, a blonde by the name of Linda shows up, and I fall in love. So, thinking I was doing the right thing, I asked Patsy for a divorce. We got the divorce, and then Linda, who was as much a predator as I was, and I broke up very, very quickly."

In 1974, he officially concluded his time inside, serving only four months of a four year sentence.

"I got out of prison with nothing," Sam says,

but he had his usual luck. "My cashier's mother managed apartment complexes where there was an opening in the nicest building they had, a ground floor apartment with sliding doors right next to the sidewalk to the parking lot. I loaded up my station wagon with boxes and bags and moved in. Now I had a nice apartment, and I filled it up with furniture. I got multiple credit cards, and I was dating often and going to movies, theater and ball games. I spent on anything and everything, just gotta have this and that, and was living way beyond my means. I was a six-year old kid in a candy store — zero sense. By the time the court tracked me down for child support, I'd been out 12 or 18 months, and I was bankrupt already. When I had to fill out some court forms, I had more due in credit card payments than income.

"In 1976, I was managing a convenience store, and a woman named Missy came in. I am not noted for this, but about the second time she came into the store, what popped out of my mouth was 'Would you go on a date with me tonight?'

"We began dating, and I ramped things up and moved her out of her alcoholic dad's place and in with me, and we were married in about four months. With most of the women I've known, I've been distinctly the bad apple, but in this case, she was more of a bad apple than I was, and that was a rare thing. Missy began working part-time at the store, and I have no doubt she was having sex with other guys while I was working. One of those guys, an ex-con who was hanging around, stole checks from my register, too. She was just as much a user of people as I was.

"My life had always been like that, no sense of intuition that is the spiritual connection; it's all about me, and I'm blind to others. I went to a counselor friend and whined for days about Missy, and he finally said to me, 'You picked her.' So I reviewed my relationships with women: every one of them failed, and I was the constant.

"Missy wanted a horse, so even though I was living on credit cards, I bought her an Arabian and got myself a Morgan. We moved to a trailer in the country with five acres of land around it that I rented from some farmers. I built a shed for the horses, but there was no water supply. It was a mess, especially in winter when we had to haul buckets of water out there. I would not ask anyone how to raise horses or put up a fence because I never asked for advice or insight or help.

"The situation with Missy from beginning to end was a disaster. It was over in 22 months, and she moved out. She came and took her horse when I was not home, and I gave mine away. It hurt, but more in a control and loneliness way, along with some of that fear of abandonment and shame. I felt 'how could you do this to me?' the same thing I practiced on other people."

SEVEN

Fire, and Then...

S am was and is a book lover, and he also writes for himself with no specific purpose in mind.

"It is more an emotional than a thoughtful thing," he told me, "like letting air out of the soul so you don't get overwhelmed."

He'd remember something about Vietnam "or this and that" and pound out paragraphs about it. He would get insights, make a one or two sentence note and flesh an essay out weeks later—if he could decipher the scribbles. It surprised me to learn this, because I do the same thing, never quite catching up with my stacks of fragmentary ideas sketched on receipts, church bulletins or even the back of my hand, and largely all of them unreadable later.

Over the seasons, as we met at his home, new shelves a friend made for him appeared along his living room walls. They were not filling up with books, however. I noticed the music boxes were proliferating. His swelling collection of sweet and silly things is the consequence of Sam's prowls through Goodwill and Salvation Army stores.

"I pretty much cleaned them out," he announced to me one day as we poured coffee before we began recording. "I got something for you, too." He handed me a Lemony Snicket blank writing journal with neatly ruled pages, just the right size to carry around. As he had said when we talked about his childhood, he always tried to be thoughtful about gift giving. He'd gotten it right, and I felt touched, just as I had when he told me that he and Missy had owned horses. They're my deepest passion, and I had mentioned to Sam a bit about my own horses. Early on I wondered if I were getting unprofessionally close to my subject. Is he a kind and unusually well-read con-man? I could cite more than a few instances where journalists have been sucked in by prisoners or deceived by former prisoners while writing a book about them.

Sam's candor was clear and seems genuine to me largely because of his long dedication to a 12 Step program that encourages complete honesty. I decided not to refuse his gifts or withhold my own stories.

His love of books and his personal writing were not enough to keep Sam out of trouble after the first prison and his second divorce. He was no longer drinking, but he was unable to behave himself in healthy ways with women.

"I got fired from the convenience store for patting cashiers on the butt, so I started working for a guy doing painting and sheet rock," he said. "One day, he and I stopped for a burger at a café, and I met Julie, a new waitress there. A day or two later asked her out."

There were warning signs: her children Lucy, six, and Teddy, four, were not fathered by her husband or even by the same man.

By mid-winter, Julie and Sam had been dating about four months. He was living in the 12' by 60' trailer house on top of a half basement with a woodstove. The farmers who owned the trailer had done the wiring themselves, and Joe was going to re-wire it, because he noticed something had torqued the aluminum wiring and loosened the nuts in the outlets and light switches.

"One December night, there was a blizzard, and when I got home from shingling, it was bitterly cold," he said, "I threw some wood in the stove and got it going, and I'm sitting in the bathtub upstairs. I lay back and figured what I see in the bathroom is just moisture in the air. Then — what's that smell? That smell is wood!

"I put on my slippers and bathrobe and opened the door to the basement, and here was a ring of fire above the elbow of the stove. I grabbed the itty-bitty fire extinguisher and sprayed it, but it roared back to life. I pulled down the fake ceiling, and the sub floor was flickering in flames, so I ran over and turned on the pressure tank valve for the hose — no water. I ran upstairs to call the fire department — the phone was dead. My briefcase, which contained pens and cigarettes and eight dollars in my wallet, was lying on the table. I managed to find that, and I got out and drove up to the neighbors' place. They gave me a flannel shirt and jeans, and I called the fire department, but the place was gone. My books, my writing, everything was burned up, so I drove to Julie's apartment.

"I'm sure people thought that I probably started that fire myself, because I'm a ne'er-do-well. Then I went on to call my lawyer and file bankruptcy.

"Shortly after that I went out Christmas shopping and bought fire extinguishers for all my family and friends. We went to Dad's for Christmas where they were not well received. To them, the fire and the fire extinguishers were one more stupid thing Sam had done.

"A couple weeks later, I got laid off from the construction job, so I became a house husband. Julie had a half-day job at a restaurant, so although she wanted to be a housewife, I ended up taking over, not intentionally. I did laundry and made meals, both not well. We ate a lot of macaroni.

"Out in the country there was not a lot to do once I had cleaned the house and put a meal in the oven. I would get tired of TV, but I love Legos, they are simplistic, like crossword puzzles, and I saw to it that Teddy always got Legos at Christmas. So in the morning, after Julie went to work and the kids went to school, I'd call myself up and tell myself I was not coming to work today, and I'd play Legos. While I had been locked up in prison, I wanted a safe place, and the idea of a sanctuary grew in my mind, a utopia were people could co-exist. I was fervent about that, and years later, I even picked out a spot for it, something fireproof with south exposure. During those days at home, I would build this thing out of Legos."

Being a house husband was in no way adequate stimulation or action for him, Legos or not. A mind like Sam's—uneducated but searching— and the energy he had then as well as a need for more money for the family moved him to get back to full time work.

"I was working a little shingling and decided I need to do something different. A gas station manager job came open, and they only hired married couples, so Julie and I married six months after we met. I hired her to work at the station, and when I got a job selling insurance, she moved up to manager."

Sam played the role of family provider fairly well, selling insurance successfully around a cluster of states. He ran enrollment seminars at large state and corporate institutions where he successfully sold new programs and products to thousands of employees. He used his natural sociability and persuasiveness in other ways as well including playing Santa Claus during the holidays. He really wanted to create that *Father Knows Best* life he'd seen as a kid on TV.

"For a few years, I played Santa Claus quite a bit. I did it for Amicus gatherings and for the mayor's chief of staff. I wore a white wig and beard, I had the boots, Julie made me a custom Santa suit, and I had a large bag of candy to give away. Julie made outfits for herself and the kids, too, and they sometimes went along as helpers. Parents would make arrangements for me to come to their house beforehand and collect their kids' gifts, then I could hand them out. It was a pretty good gig and fun.

"It was a challenge to have a reason why Santa was there that kiddies would believe. I had to come up with a story, so I would say, 'I am knocking on your front door looking for one of my reindeer — that sneaky Rudolph has slipped out of his harness and taken off.' I had some leather and bells that I would show them.

"They'd ask me, 'How will you know when he comes back?' At a novelty store I'd found a small stainless steel ball that chimed if you twisted it. The little ones would sit on my knee and hold my hand, and I'd hold the ball. I told them I'd know when the reindeer are near when the ball chimes. Older people were scoffers — it's not gonna chime — but when sweat started running down my nose in that suit indoors, and all the scoffers were scoffing, I'd give it a twist, and suddenly chimmmmmme!

"There was a house near the river that was all lit up with holiday lights, and sometimes I'd stop there, and the guy would give me a bag of candy. I'd stand outside the home and greet people for two to three hours and do the Santa thing. It was cold, but it was so much fun to bring joy to people. I never charged money, it was a blast, and we did a good job and made a lot of people happy."

Meanwhile, despite some material comforts, Sam's family was not so happy.

"I knew Julie wasn't emotionally well, and I knew she had suffered. Her mom and dad had littered their house with a dozen kids, probably not unique to Catholics, because the more kids you have the holier you are, but how the hell do you have time to live or to love them? With Julie, if you're just a kid, you don't count.

"So her daughter Lucy was no part of Julie's life, and Lucy was distant from me as well, because I'm just one more man who's coming into the house, but now I'm staying. Lucy was distant, and I think that was a consequence of having discovered that who she thought was her father was not her father. Maybe you don't know that as a seven-year old child, but it's a miasma around you. She spent her time basically in her room, reading probably. Lucy was on her own.

"As a parent, I really wanted the kids to experience more than I had. We got them in band at school and in T-ball and softball. We went fishing, to the beach and swimming more than anybody in Julie's family had done. We took the kids to California, camped, and then worked our way down the Pacific Coast. I took them to regional theatre, exposed them to things like that which people from rural areas are not involved in, and we did normal family stuff like amusement parks and baseball games. We played Candyland and Bingo and, of course, Legos.

"Ted was a pretty warm and friendly kid, so there would be a sincere hug from him, but it wasn't there from Lucy. I had expectations that she was going to be a loving daughter, but there was this wall. It was like walking down an aisle in a store, just, 'Hi, how you doin', glad to see you,' and we'd pass the time about the weather and go on about our business.

"I thought I was being personal with Julie and with Patsy and with other women in my life, but I wasn't. It was alien to me. I didn't know how to have it, but I wanted it. And then, of course, there's that dictatorial thing that's part of me being distant, and I had to be distant from people, so with Lucy it was, 'Damn it, I thought I told you to clean your room!'"

I knew the specifics of Sam's criminal record, I knew what was coming, and I knew he would not shirk to tell me the details. I could sit through hearing it without stopping him or criticizing him, because during decades as a newspaper and magazine reporter interviewing literally thousands of people, I'd heard incredible stuff, both glorious and ghastly, much more from victims than from perpetrators. With notable exceptions that include Sam, perpetrators usually don't want their stories told, and for obvious good reasons. Sam told me repeatedly he did not need a book about his recovery, that he was actually indifferent to it. He agreed to collaborate on this work, he said "because it could help someone else who was lost." Thus after weeks of conversation with him, I felt prepared to hear what he was going to reveal. I knew he would give it his trademark thoughtful, unadorned description. And over more coffee, he pressed on to what we both knew was the hardest, most soul-scorching part of his story.

"And then... I would go to prison this last time for sexually abusing Lucy," Sam said quietly. "I wanted to be intimate, and I don't mean sexually, but that was the only thing I knew. I wanted affection, but I didn't know how to get it, how to look for it, how to give it.

"I never once got up in the morning and looked at Lucy and said, 'I'm going to have sex with her,' and I honestly don't remember what triggered what. In the rat's nest of my imagination I thought maybe she'll feel closer to me if we're intimate in some way. Whatever it was, the excuse was an alibi for me, and that's all there was to it.

"I wanted affection, kindness, love, respect, but what the hell? I'm an emotional child myself, and the only way I knew how to relate to a female was that way. Somewhere in there, sadly, I didn't think of Lucy. To me, at that time, she was an object, and seeing her that way kept me from having to deal with reality and feeling pain and consequences.

"Believe it or not, I think I did it based in some type of love. For so many years I was right on the edge of crazy, but it was the only way I knew how to be — that edge of sane madness. What do they call that? There's a good psychiatric term for it, sociopath or something.

"It played out in more ways, like I was not faithful to Julie. I never once woke up in the morning and said, 'I want to be bad, dumb, stupid, or evil,' but I could be sitting at a bar, and a woman's husband is sitting right there with us, and I'm making coy remarks to her that I think

I can get away with. Or I'd tell myself that this woman is not married or this won't bother her, or this is just a one-time thing.

"At the time, I had no ability to step back and reflect, and I didn't have these words — sociopath, for example.

"When you've taken someone's life, and it did not bother you at all, then nothing is sacred, nothing and no one, except the satiation of your emotions: me with a box cutter and I'm going to kill a woman. Me with my first wife and friends in the car and I was going to run somebody down, because I'm mad. I was perhaps not certifiable, but I was crazy. I didn't plan these things. Something just snapped.

"Lucy was just a child and had nobody except the two people who should take care of her. The abuse was occasional, not every day, but in the meantime, she had a roof over her head, wonderful Christmases and vacations, and in my mind, I could use these things to justify my actions. Every time with Lucy I promised myself, 'I'm not going to do this again.' There was a shred of guilt there. Lucy became simply compliant, as she had learned to be, to shut up, eat, give a peck on the cheek, go to bed, get up and go to school.

"Of course, there was no love and affection in it, and so now I'm angry, and then there would be this snowball effect and a tirade from me.

"Julie knew to a degree that it was happening, and I knew it was going to end someday, but it's kind of like knowing about lung cancer and choosing to have one more cigarette. Meanwhile, Ted didn't mean much to any of us. Julie, Lucy and I were involved in our own sick world. Ted was not an impediment. Sadly, we just ignored him.

"This went on for almost six years, until Lucy was 17, and then Julie and Lucy finally had a heart-to-heart talk. There were a couple items that couldn't be explained away: Lucy knew this, Julie knew that, they both didn't know it all, and then they knew.

"Julie told me she was going to the police. I became profoundly suicidal. I only knew how to cope with things by running away, which I did."

Sam was so deeply ashamed at that point that he was prepared to more than run away from their home. He was preparing to run away from life itself.

FOUND

Six Apples

Things were about to get better for him through a simple gesture, although when he fled their house, Sam could not anticipate that.

Julie indeed called the police, while Sam sped away. He drove to the riverside parking lot of a rural lock and dam where he first thought about putting a chili can on his exhaust pipe or shooting himself. Then he changed — not his mind but his method of suicide.

"It was an egotistical thing," he told me. "I didn't want some son of a bitch thinking that in a moment of despair I offed myself. I wanted people to know I chose suicide not in a tantrum but purposely and intentionally, that I was in charge.

"I decided that dying those ways was too fast. Then I had the idea to starve myself to death, so I sat in my broken-down station wagon for twenty-two days and didn't eat. At first I drank milk, then I switched to water, because I realized I was putting calories in my body. I was thinking about punishment, about prison time and about all those who would put me there. I was thinking 'You bastards! You are not gonna make me do something I don't want to do, I'm going to do things my way!' Although I had been the guy who didn't give a damn, I definitely was tired of who I was, I didn't want to be here anymore. And as for the dying, it isn't the physical part I feared, it's that you're so full of pain that you numb yourself from caring, and then you have a living death.

"Every day some guys would meet there

at the dam to fish, and one of them, an older guy named Harvey, suspected something. I was parked in the same place every day, he'd come over, and we got talking. One day Harvey showed up with a bag of six apples. After he left, I secretly threw them in the trash. The next day when he asked me if I had enjoyed them I lied to him.

"Soon it dawned on Mr. No Conscience — me — the kind man Harvey was. It may sound trivial, but it was a door opener for empathy and caring. I was dipping my toes into the water of humanity for the first time. I would have felt dishonorable if I threw the apples away again, and up to that point, I didn't feel that way about anybody or anything. Now I couldn't stand the thought of lying to him again. That is a seemingly inconsequential thing, but I had a feeling, there was still a spark of humanity inside me. Otherwise I was devoid of most human emotions.

"Next time Harvey gave me some apples,

I ate them all, because he was going to come back and ask me about it, and I would not lie to him. I felt cleaner. Now I really didn't want to hurt people any more. That was a unique feeling for me."

In starvation, Sam told me, the body takes the fat last. He was pretty muscular back then, and he didn't notice a lot of weight going away. He spent a fair amount of time listening to the car radio, and whenever a tow boat came through the lock, and he'd watch the process. Mostly, he suffered.

"When I started being self-destructive at that lock and dam, I was full of fear, anger, hopelessness, rage, helplessness, and pretty much lost. Even if you are a crook you feel crapped on, it's all about me and I only know how to be destructive. After three weeks of living in my car and eating apples, a little bit of the truth crept in, and I realized how wrong I was. I did care about Lucy, Teddy and Julie, but I didn't know how to. I really did care about the kids — they had done nothing wrong. Julie was an adult, and she'd been doing her stuff too, and she was more of an acter-outer. We were users of each other, and I had less tender, youthful, innocent feelings for her. The older I get the more I have empathy for her, because I recognize the depth of her despair and the endlessness of it."

Each time I sat with or called Sam, I heard more details of episodes from his childhood to his present life, and it took me several hearings of this story to understand that the place he began to move from lost to found was in the parking lot on the river. Harvey and his apples seemed small but proved to be significant.

"It dawned on me there 'I can't do this,'" he continued. "I use the word epiphany quite a bit, and to me it is just awareness, not Christ comes down from heaven. Unless we entirely close ourselves off, awareness comes. Unless we go raving mad, it can come. And then what am I going to do with it? Sometimes it is a slow process and sometimes it takes a few hours, sometimes a few years. It is not coordinated or in order. We always are challenged to be open to change, even though we create little worlds for ourselves so we don't have challenges."

Then, instead of continuing to starve alone in his car, Sam called Joe from a phone booth in the area and told him where he was.

"He dropped what he was doing and met me. We sat and talked, and I made a commitment to turn myself in. We drove into town, and then, still not being very wise, I ended up having a great big 12-inch hot dog that made me sick for a week. We drove to Joe's home the next day, where the sheriff arrived and seized my car and me."

Change or Die

The trial took two or three days, then Sam was convicted of child sexual abuse and sentenced to 15 years. He was sitting in the county jail in a five by eight feet cell containing a steel cot with a lousy mattress. Sam was still despairing, although far down inside he was changing. The gift of the apples, he tells me, was the turning point for him, although plenty of drama was to follow.

"I lied my way through the trial," he said, flatly. "I would stand in front of the judge, my wife, my parents, whoever, and lie. I understood that they were angry, I understood that they were upset, but I did not understand the wrongness of what I had done. I don't know if the word is psychotic or psychosis or what the medical terms are, but there was just this wall up in me at that time, and prisons are full of men like me.

"The first meal they served in that jail had some stuff that I used to fashion a lethal weapon. I still wanted to destroy myself. A few days later, I made a backup weapon and hid that one as well. I didn't know exactly when I was going to be transported from jail to a prison, and I was not going to be able to take these with me. A week or two later, I knew I needed to make the decision.

"One night about a week or ten days after sentencing, I'm leaning there against the bars of my bunk, and I have my left hand up in the air — this is not the normal me — and all of the sudden, the words 'God' and 'love' pop into my head. I resolved at that moment to go to prison and for the rest of my life treat each person I met from there on out with as much love and respect as possible. I destroyed the two lethal items I had made and sat and waited for other people to make the decision. I just accepted. I was not a spiritual or a godly person, but I opened the door wide — I didn't realize how wide — for the will of God. I didn't think of those words at the time, but I became willing to do whatever it took to be a spiritual person rather than me. I was not going to be whoever I had been anymore, ever. Until then, there was nothing I ever followed through on that was decent or righteous, nothing, not with any human being that I can think of. For once in my life, after I got convicted, I had to change or die. I didn't understand at that moment real well, but I knew this wasn't religion. It was something spiritual, an awakening.

"A deputy sheriff drove me in a patrol car, handcuffed, to a receiving prison. They take you in, you take a shower, and they issue clothes. You put on one set of clothes, throw the rest in a bag, and they put you in a holding cell where there's a toilet and a sink and a concrete bench. The guard pushed me in the door, and all these guys were already there and no place for me to sit. Most of these guys had been in prison a number of times, including a guy nicknamed Martello, one of the few human beings I've seen in my life who not only looks like but sounds like a convict — all scarred up, with a real tough-looking face. (His nickname means hammer in Italian.) I'm standing there feeling outnumbered, and he looks at me and growls 'Grrrrrr! Who are you, and what are you in here for?' Who the hell wants to tell him I'm here for sex abuse of a child? So I broke a promise to myself and, out of fear, lied right away and said assault.

"Later on, when they took us into a wing, Martello's cell was across the hallway from mine. The facility used to be an old mental hospital, and the cells had a window and a trap that could be opened for food trays, books or papers you had to sign. In that area, there was Wally, Tommy, Martello and me. We would all go to chow together down the hallway to the canteen. It was a place of transition while the county decided which prison they were sending you to. There was not much to do: we would read, write letters, take naps, or sit around.

"This went on for a few weeks, then we got transferred to another Midwest prison. Tommy got sent there a day or two ahead of us. He heard that Martello and Wally were coming so we talked to the guards and lobbied for us to be near each other. We'd tell them, 'Sarge, that guy is a really good guy, he's not a troublemaker,' and we ended up having this little network.

"Mostly they played cards, and sometimes Martello and Nick sat there for eight straight hours playing cribbage. It was a battle, and the same way with cards, they were serious about it. It was an ego thing, a male macho thing. I wouldn't do that, but I'd snap at them, 'There's 15 reasons for playing cards, and only one of them is important, and that's sharing time with another person.'

"There were some unseen benefits to me because of who I associated with. I don't doubt for a minute if it wasn't for Martello, I may not have made it through my first three years in prison. Just who he was, just his presence, helped. Martello was a mafia affiliate, and he really was, this old convict, a tough guy. He's doing 160 years, I don't think he's going to get parole. Then there was T-Bone, a black guy, and he was the big dog. I don't know if he was Vice Lords or the Gangster Disciples, but he and Martello were tight.

"I've still got a mouth on me, and about 18 months into my sentence, I said something to a guy in the dorm that was factually accurate but in a tone of voice to make him feel about two inches tall and there only to be stepped on. Sitting on my bunk later, I realized what I'd done was wrong. I tracked him down inside the day room and said, 'I want to apologize to you for how I said what I said.' Now, you don't do that in prison, you just don't do that. You've got to be a tough guy. You don't cry, you don't show vulnerability or people will take advantage. There's a pecking order in prison, but I found a way that I could be me. I chose my words carefully there. Apologizing was my first step towards kindness and toward not rationalizing my continuing to be evil anymore. I was no longer spiritually dead. I was making some changes in my life and was willing to make more.

"That prison has a large sleeping area dorm and a smaller day room. One night, I grabbed an 80-page tablet, my radio, coffee mug, and an ashtray and walked into the day room. I started doodling on the tablet, and I was thinking there's got to be some reason for how things work, how people behave. There's got to be something. The pen just started flowing Monday night. At about 8:00 or 8:30 p.m. on Friday night, it stopped, and I had filled page after page after page — four 80-page tablets. I'd never written so much in my life in such a short time.

"I realized there's all this stuff about love, generosity, righteousness, patriotism and everything else, but what everybody is controlled by is fear. Everybody talks about Jesus and love, but our operational basis comes from fear and how we cope with fear. We cope through material things. Food, sex, money and geography are ways we define ourselves: Who I'm with and where I am living. We're afraid we're not going to have, do or get what we want or we will get things we don't want. I recognized 19 areas of human conflict, and what they have in common is human emotions. We live in our emotions and are not even aware of it. Finally, this started to make sense to me.

"Pride is a big part of our behavior. Convicts know their names, crimes, prison number and the word 'respect.' In prison I heard the word 'respect' so much I became sick of it. Pride can mean instead of looking at yourself, it's what the naughty judge did to you — 'He did not treat me with respect.' I know now, years later, that whenever I am disturbed, I am the one responsible. People need to look inside. We don't know how to look inside. We don't want to, and that is spiritually, emotionally and socially deadly.

"I sealed the four tablets in manila envelopes and mailed them out to Joe. He was holding my property, and I asked him not to open the envelopes.

"Not long after I did that the midwest prison started shipping prisoners from my prison to the South. The midwestern and northern prisons were out of room and needed to save money, so they did some contracts with a for-profit prison corporation. It's warehousing, nothing more. I dodged that bullet for quite a while, but I finally got tagged to go to Mississippi."

TEN

Deep South Chaos

Sam told me often, "If you're going to commit a crime, make damn sure you do it in the North or Midwest, because these other states are hellholes for prisoners."

He has reason to know from his years behind the bars of five different penal institutions. The time Sam served in the South also propelled him into action putting his natural writing skills to good use to benefit himself and his fellow prisoners.

"It was a long, miserable ride down there to 'Ode to Billie Joe' country where that particular prison is run by the Corrections Corporation of America (CCA), the evilest people on the face of the earth. On the prison bus I was cuffed to another guy, two by two. We got to the CCA facility and they unloaded us and put us in our pods. I had been in a dorm, now we were all in a cell block or a pod and two-man cell. Things started getting bad right away. They implied everything was supposedly on a schedule, but in actuality there was no schedule.

"It would start at 8:00 a.m. with the guards screaming into the dorm, 'Get up! Get this place clean!' but we had no cleaning supplies. They wouldn't be brought until an hour later. In the chow hall, you're talking rice and beans. By law, you have 15 minutes to eat your meal, but in four minutes the guards were pounding on the table for us to hurry up and finish.

"There were tables with chess and checker grids, but there was no card playing in that prison. Guards were stealing food out of the refrigerator in the kitchen, so at night the cook would lock the walk-in refrigerator. After the milk sat out for 12 to 15 hours, it always tasted sour.

"Everything was unpredictable there. When you got your food or clothing. When you went to the library. When or if you got to rec. It was just chaos.

"They had a prison library, a really small one, but half the books were first grade or second grade reading level. People there can't read, and I mean the guards, too, not just prisoners. Northern prisons have a sense of education, but they don't have that in Mississippi. And Mississippi wasn't an exception. A friend of mine who was in another southern prison told me his job was to fill out the reports for the staff because they couldn't read.

"My cellie was reading *Star Trek* books, and I was grabbing other stuff, when I could. I might find one sentence in a Zane Grey book or maybe two or three paragraphs, and

I would faithfully copy those and put in the punctuation. Even in *Star Trek* books I would find something by Spock or Kirk, and I'd copy those down. I eventually ended up with a 12-point rating system for the books I read. The low was a frown emoticon and the high was 10 stars. I often got something of value even from lesser-starred books, things like loving your wife, and she dies and you save her wedding ring, but it's what's inside that you got from her rather than the wedding ring that matters.

"I created a book list and the ratings were good reminders for me. What became important to me are the hundreds of pages of laboriously hand-copied passages from books and articles that I found significant. The notes on the books were all I had, and they were precious to me.

"When we asked for something in that CCA-run Tallahatchee prison we gave it a week, then 10 days, then two weeks. Nothing, there was no organization. We couldn't even get toilet paper, and we're talking about a two- to three-week period. I started writing down the times that I asked for a roll of toilet paper and the date and who I asked. The supervisor came around one day, and I caught up with her on the tier, and I said, 'We need toilet paper. I told the guard I need a roll of toilet paper or some more clean t-shirts, because me and my cellie are going to start wiping our butts with them.'

"She told me all we had to do is ask. I said, 'Here's the names of the guards with the times and dates that I have already asked them.' After that, she had toilet paper delivered to my cell, and that's real nice, but what about everybody else?

"The assistant warden hauled me down to his office repeatedly, because I was a fount of information for him. I would tell him straight out, without cussing and swearing, what was going on. 'Oh no, that can't be,' he'd say, 'I can't believe that. This will be taken care of, don't you worry.' He knew it was all true. It was illegal and a travesty, but nothing changed. Of course, the white shirts—the supervisors — would come around and promise, 'We'll take care of it, we'll take care of it.' But nothing changed.

"One inmate told them, 'To hell with you, this is the law, this is my right,' and they threw him in a pod all by himself. They did that so he could have no communication with anybody else.

"After about four or five weeks of this, I wrote 48 letters in 60 days to Amnesty International, the FBI, Mississippi DOC (Department of Corrections), other state DOCs, any TV stations, radio stations, newspapers, anybody I could tell what was going on in that prison. I didn't want to be thrown in the hole by myself, but it was something I felt I gotta do for the rest of us. I was scared to death, because in northern prisons when you seal a letter they mail it for you. But in the South, we were required to leave letters open. It turns out they weren't reading all the mail anyway.

"As a kind of safety net, I also wrote my Amicus friend Joe and told him what I'd done. He was the only outside person I knew I could do that with, and I wanted someone to know what I was doing. There was the possibility that if the guards or the warden didn't like it, I might 'accidentally' fall down a stairwell or get thrown in the hole or worse.

"One day, one of the contract monitors came around. When she came by, I ran out there and sat down at the table with her, because she was the big dog in terms of who's in charge of this prison. I started pointing at guards who protected me, so if something happens to me as a result of my campaign they would know.

"The northern prison canceled the contract with the southern prison and were pulling us out. They transferred us — all 400 men — into a 64-cell pod where we sat there for a couple days. On transfer day guys were taken out of their cells in twos with belly chains and wrist cuffs and chained together in a chair. Shackles were put on us, we went through the door to the cell block, and there was a control panel for the different pods.

"They counted us going out of the door into the hallway, they counted us a couple more times going down the hallway out to the buses, counted us repeatedly in seven busloads to Memphis where we waited on the plane for several hours. We were delayed at the airport because a guy named Ron and his cellie had been forgotten. Somebody threw these two guys in a vehicle and sneaked them into the Memphis airport past the contract monitors so they wouldn't know these people were so damn incompetent they couldn't count. That's the kind of people that we are dealing with in prisons in the United States, that's CCA.

"When I read about corrections in America and what's going to be done about it, it makes me sick. Reform? You could beat that dog, and he'll stop doing what he's doing until you're not looking, and then he just learns to be more sly. People do the only thing they know how to do."

Sam had found that prison systems, like individuals, resist change, even for the better. They take the easy way, and are in general not based on recovery, positive growth or spiritual betterment. He won't take credit for it, but without his actions, things at this particular site could have stayed awful, and no doubt they reverted after he was moved out.

In the Hole

In both southern and northern prisons, Sam found a way to live as a sort of monk. He threw himself into reading, thinking, writing and practicing the vows he had made. Although he admits it was not easy all the time, he considers that decade behind bars the best years of his life. It gave him the undistracted time to practice recovery, which began back in the county jail with his pledge to turn his life over to a higher power, to promptly admit when he was wrong, and to attend in healthy ways to others.

"Service with expectations is not service," he reminds me. "In prison, I didn't have expectations. I wasn't preachy, but I found a way that I could be a friend to some people without kissing up or without letting them take advantage of me. I was trying to be honest.

"In April 2003, I was in a damn good northern prison, and I had a good job there washing dishes at the dorm. I always like washing dishes. You've got the machine, you can take your time, and you can get extra food in the kitchen. The lead man in the kitchen was a guy named Red. He was about 80, and his grandson was in prison, too, the first time ever, working in the same unit. I was celled up with a guy I didn't particularly care for, and I thought I could do better. Red's grandson was celled up with a guy who was pretty rough, then he moved out, so I immediately moved in with Red's grandson. I had a radio and TV and stuff I could share with him, and we lived there for about a week.

"Then an officer came around doing a

shakedown, he was an irascible fellow, and when I went out and had a cigarette and came back in, uh-oh: the officer found a Kool-Aid container with about a finger of 90 proof liquid in the bottom. The grandson's former cellie had made hooch and left it there. We had nothing to do with it.

"At that point, I'd been locked up for eight and a half years, I had a stellar record, and I had done nothing to harm anybody else, but they weren't going to believe me, and they're not going to believe this new kid either. So he and I were thrown in the hole (isolation) for something we didn't do. My access to TV, radio, ink pens, books, crossword puzzle books, candy, gum and cigarettes was gone.

"I was trembling with rage. I hadn't known rage like that since I don't know when. I can't describe how quickly I went down so far so fast. I got 30 days in the hole and did 21 days in a 10 by 12 foot cell, sleeping on a concrete bench with a crappy mattress, a toilet, and an opaque window. I had reading material, writing paper and a pencil… that was it. Occasionally they would bring around some well-used library books. All you can do is read, sleep, and learn to endure. I felt very emotional about it; I was attached to my buddies and card games, and I felt some deathly frustration and rage about the unfairness. Though I was in prison, I was living large, and life was good. But all of the sudden this was unfair.

"Suddenly I realized, so was what I did to Lucy! So was what I did to steal money from my dad, so is all this other stuff, it's all unfair. But now it's happening to me. I encountered myself with no filtering, with no white washing. I had to sit there and look at myself. This is where the rubber hit the road.

"About a day or so later it dawned on me how I had depersonalized and dehumanized women. Every time I was sexually satisfying myself, who was I thinking of? I was thinking of some woman I'd already been with and every relationship had failed. Or I was thinking of some woman I'd never been with. At any rate, I had depersonalized and dehumanized every one.

"Sexism is one of the ways we empower ourselves. It's not about being adult and growing up, it's about empowering, rationalizing and justifying. Men marry women younger than them so he has the power, for example, and that's not unique to this era and country.

"I swore an oath to God that day, which I kept, that I would be celibate. I would never ask a woman on a date or hint or flirt until God saw fit to send a woman to me who asked me out. It's been dicey at moments, but I've stuck to it. It's like not smoking — it spells more freedom. Other than being celibate, there are not too many ways to demonstrate that you're crime-free and morally changed.

"When I got out of the hole, I was in a dorm. Normally prison dorms aren't good places to live, but this was, or it was better than a cell hall. It could still be a violent place — I saw a guy with his jawbone sticking out after he'd gotten beat up at the dorm.

"Once in awhile I'd meet some guy in the dorm and learn about his struggle and hardships. I could discern whether it was a lie or not, so every now and then, I'd have $15 or $20 sent to that guy anonymously just to help him out. Not too often, but occasionally. I'd already got all the treats you can have when you're locked up.

"One day after work I came back to my locker, and everything I owned was gone. My zoo-zoos and wham-whams (a prison phrase for ink pens, stamps, sodas, candy, cigarettes) were all gone. The locker was empty. Well, two other inmates nicknamed Toad and Slick Willy broke into my locker and took everything I owned. Looking at my empty locker was like being naked in church. You just don't want this, and what can you do? I walked into the day room and told Martello what happened,

and he said, 'It's your call' meaning I could decide what was going to happen for retaliation.

"You do not want to be a patsy, an easy
mark, in any prison, and these guys stole my
stuff, yet years before I had sworn an oath to
God, so I had to decide how I was going to
respond. It was the longest damn 10 to 15 minutes. The dorm was the old chow hall, so it's a
pretty good-sized building, and the day room
was about a quarter the size of the sleeping
area. Soon every inmate in the dorm was inside the day room peeking out the window at
me as I sat alone in the sleeping area.

"The three guards didn't know what the hell
was going on. I'm surprised they didn't push
a button and get the goon squad in, because
someone sitting alone while everyone else
watched meant something was up.

"I sat out there, and I remembered my oath
to God. So I got up and walked into the day
room. Martello was standing there at the big
steel door. In life, there's talking and then

there's doing. Martello was on the doing side, although he was making changes in his life. I said to him and everyone else, 'There will be no violence. I would like to have my stuff back if I can. If I cannot, that's okay,' and I turned around and walked out.

"I got everything back that had been stolen and more, and from that day forward, the prison changed. The Aryan Brotherhood, the Gangster Disciples and all the other gangs declared the dorm off limits for everything. All the crimes that they normally do to each other stopped, and for two years, that became the holiest place on earth because people were sharing and caring. When people would leave, including me, you'd have anywhere from two to 10 guys on the line on the ramp hugging and saying goodbye, There were even tears. It was fabulous.

"It's what God wanted for that place. Sometimes He allows evil, because we have to have something to balance.

"There are some good men in prison, not too many, but you do find some. You also find some good guards, some that you'd want to spend the rest of your life with. They're just decent human beings. Others get corrupted by the system. Well, who do you trust in there? It's not easy to know. You naturally start becoming a little steely or a little distant, distrustful, suspicious or guarded.

"Guards were one reason the dorm was nice: Matt and Monroe were the day cops at the front desk area, and Jack was the door guard. You're with these people for two to three years eight hours a day, and you can develop a relationship. A relationship has got a thousand different definitions, but there's an element of trust between inmates and guards sometimes.

"On one anniversary of the prison, they administration allowed some civilians to come into the building on tours. I looked up at the observation level above us, and there were two little kids with a couple of adults looking down into our dorm. There were inmates changing clothes or sitting in their underwear, and that seemed wrong. I felt like an animal in a cage anyway, but it was too much with the kids watching us. I went into the day room, got a form, filled it out, signed my name (which was scary) and put it in the suggestion box. The next morning the sergeant — the good guy — said to me, 'We got a problem here.' Instead of hauling me to the hole, however, he calls Matt over and asks me, 'Sam, what can we do about this?' He assured me it would not happen again. That's not unique to me and that time in prison — there's opportunities like that all the time in life.

"In prison, there's no other way to say it, though I met some badass people, and I had some hairy moments, but dammit, they were the best ten years of my life. It was like Vietnam where everybody else around me was all screwed up, dying or what have you, but I remained untouched. It was the first time I'd consistently been around people for any real length of time, and I started to appreciate who and what they were becoming rather than what they had been. I didn't even know what most guys were in prison for because I never asked.

"By the time I was eligible for parole, through the ability to start being discerning about the people I met there and all the books I read, I had been through a form of college.

"After 10 years, through five prisons, I had devoured more than 800 books or about 36,000 pages. I read one three times — *Many Lives, Many Masters* by Dr. Brian Weiss. From all these books, I made a couple of three-ring binders of handwritten notes where I had copied significant sentences, paragraphs or pages to partially embed perspectives. During that time, I grew to realize we are an intelligent species, but mostly lacking in wisdom, as that is a process, not an endowment.

'The prison librarian used to bring me all

the newspapers every day, and I'd go through them all. I read the local paper, the state-wide paper and even *USA Today*. I would go through the news, clipping out articles and thinking why do we as people do the things we do? Why in God's name would a bank teller embezzle money? Why did that wealthy guy in the big lake home shoot his wife and kids? Why do we do this stuff?

"So you sit there and scratch your head and think how stupid, how stupid... and then I recognized the role of fear: I'm not going to get what I do want, something's going to happen I don't want. It's that simple. When I recognize I'm not going to get my way, I use pride, anger, greed, gluttony, lust, envy or sloth, all well-rationalized, justified and habitual to accomplish me getting what I want. The realization was eye-opening for me.

"The Department of Justice psychologists got all this mental jargon and it's not based in reality. They don't know what they're talking about.

"I didn't start practicing recovery until I was sitting in prison and wanted to start growing. I was in a 12 Step program and I learned how we really operate. I understand there are organic, biological issues in brains in all of us, but sometimes we just need a simplified 12 Step model rather than 36 months of counseling twice a week with words that are 20 letters long. We just need to grow up.

"In the last prison I was in, when my sentence was ending, I asked my case manager if I could do five more years, and I meant it. He chuckled and told me 'Get out of here.' The second time I went to tell him, he didn't chuckle so much, and told me to 'Get out of here' again. The third time, he got pissed off, because he figured I was harassing him. But I really didn't want to leave. I was afraid that I would succumb to the world once again. I didn't realize that muscle, physical or moral, requires resistance, an opposing force, in order to grow.

"Pre-prison, I was totally non-spiritual. I loved no one including myself. It was a preferable way of living. It was a familiar way of living. Inside prison I'd found a way to live where I was at peace. I was not harmful to myself or other people, and I was afraid when I got out that I would succumb to God-only-knows-what. I didn't want to lose what I had gained. Not so much women, but I was afraid of the ego and greed and backsliding into my pre-prison way of thinking.

"I hadn't been on the street for 10 years, and I worried about little things, too — how was I going to cope? They don't tell you a damn thing when you get out of prison. You don't know where to go or what to do. You don't know if you have a support network or will be subjected to typical bullshit groups you have to go through. After you live productively in a spiritual way, are you going to find other people to help you keep growing and changing?

"All the DOC really knows is who you were and what you did. They don't know who you are or who you have become. They don't want to, because a lot of us are slick with the tongue, we got a halo around us, we are repeat offenders. Then a child gets abused again, a woman gets raped or a car gets stolen. The job of a PO (parole officer) and police is to be very, very suspicious.

"I knew something special had happened to me in terms of understanding how I became who I was. In prison I had grown to know virtuous living, love and respect and decency and fraternity, all the positive things. I would be leaving behind some friends and men who were really significant to me.

"When I was released from prison in December, I cried every step of the way from my cell building down to Administration then every step of the way to the segregation area where the transport was. I was leaving behind men who loved me and men who I loved.

Guys came out of the buildings as I walked by, one friend here, two there, and we'd hug. We weren't supposed to do that, because you're not supposed to fraternize with people walking by your buildings, but we did it anyway.

"Your boxes of stuff are all packed up, guards throw it on the prison van, nobody talks to you, and then the prison van delivers you somewhere. All you know is you're going back to your county of conviction.

"Most people who get out have family or someone. They've been in and out of the system for a long time, and they know how it works. Not me. I saved every letter I got in prison, and not one person from my family ever wrote to me in those 10 years. I had no idea what awaited me, but I knew there was no one."

Sam told me all this without a note of self-pity, in the same even tone and tempo he had used over the previous months when he talked about serving in Vietnam, about his childhood home, his parents, his girlfriends and wives. His smoker's rumble never varied much. In answer to my questions at times he paused, contemplated silently and then spoke without ornamentation. It was all voiced with an honesty as close to a confession as I've ever heard from anyone.

TWELVE

Everybody Serves

The van delivered Sam to a small town, to a boarding house that had nine rooms populated primarily, he found, by probationers, other parolees and what he calls ne'er-do-wells.

It wasn't much, yet after a decade of confinement that had given him fundamental structure and freedom from mundane daily decisions, it was a dramatic change for Sam. He had a parole officer to report to periodically, his Amicus friends Joe and Joy checked on him and there were recovery meetings in the area as well.

"One window of my room faced the parking lot and a gully with trees," he recalled. "From the back porch, I could see a grocery store and small town streets, while out front there was a church.

"That first Christmas, I was sitting at the rooming house watching people go to late evening services, and I kind of wanted to be there, harkening back to days of youth. Christmas is a lonely time. When you're in prison, at least you had a couple of friends you can share some chips with or something.

"It took two or three weeks after they released me, then the DOC let me go to 12 Step meetings. I'd walk downtown to them, and I never missed one. My focus was not on cars, sex, drugs, R&R (what the military calls Rest and Recuperation), it was to continue the path I'd been on, so I craved recovery meetings. I was dedicated to finally growing up spiritually.

"I continued to read a lot. I read every book

to do with 12 Step programs, and 12 Step people started coming to visit me at the boarding house. We'd smoke and drink coffee together. It was like learning at the feet of elders, soaking up wisdom from people on the same path.

"Joe was storing what little property I had, and I couldn't wait for him and Joy to come visit. I wanted those manila envelopes I had mailed him years earlier. Somehow I knew instinctively they contained my salvation.

"Joe has been the 'significant other' in my life. I'd do anything for that man and his wife. It's nice to have somebody you care that much about. I've interrupted his plans a number of times, especially in my earlier years. Having me in his life has not always been convenient for him, but he's the role model I needed but never had.

"I never knew what a friend was until Joe. Joe will be there for you, unlike me. If it's inconvenient for me or I decide I don't like you or I'm going a different direction, you can hit the road. In my world, love was situational.

"Three or four months after I was paroled and living in the boarding house, Joe and Joy came to visit. When they left, I started opening up the boxes they brought and spent a couple of days sorting through them. I found those manila envelopes, opened one, but it looked like a bunch of gibberish, so I sealed it and put it away. I found my original 12 Step books that I'd been given in 1973, which I'd read one time. I started reading them again and I began to see things that were familiar: Where have I seen this before? Oh my God, where have I seen that before? All of the sudden I realized much of it — sometimes word for word, sometimes conceptually — was everything in those manila envelopes that were sealed since 1997.

"You could call it an angel whispering in your ear, God talking to you or channeling. I don't know what it is, but there's more than just me and you, there's more than meets the eye. Those 400 pages of automatic writing had

flowed through me on five successive eve-
nings. I'd had no 12 Step books at that time,
and much of what came out of me was recovery material that I had seen 20 years before if
ever.

"As for daily life, the community didn't want
a notorious sex offender like me around town.
For doctor visits. the DOC set me up through
the Veterans Administration (VA), and I went
over on the VA bus for my healthcare. Appointments are staggered throughout the day,
and what are you going to do in the meantime,
roam the hallways? They've got a smoking
shack there, so I went out to the shack between
appointments. There are people of various
ages in there, and some of the guys have a vest
on that says Airborne, or Death From Above
or When I Die I'm Going to Heaven Because
I've Already Been in Hell.

"I'm sitting there listening to these guys
talk about all their experiences in Vietnam of
partying, whoring, truck driving and the night

they heard a barrage on the green line or what have you, but they've never been there, done nothing. They were cooks, clerks, truck drivers, wannabes. I'm one of the few people that have actually experienced combat who will talk about it; most guys don't. When I came home from the VA, I'm feeling arrogant and being prideful, because I know I've got a chest full of medals. A Veterans' Services officer told me one time, 'There's 5,000 to 6,000 Vietnam vets in this county, and I think you've got more medals than anybody we've served in the county.' I found that hard to believe.

"All my medals were lost when my house burned down, so I got out an American Legion magazine, found a company you can write to, and I ordered a copy of everything that I'd been awarded. Then I took the little pins and put them on this hat, stuffed this sucker on my head, and at my next VA appointment, I went strutting down there. Then I realized that was pride in me and recognized everybody serves.

"These days, I believe pride is the first and most easily corrupting of the seven deadly sins. Pride gives me permission to do what I want to do to those around me, so I purposely wear this hat now in humility, a reminder of those who gave their lives, the real heroes. The other thing that keeps me humble is my prison coffee mug: that, happily, has never seen soap, and as long as I live, it never will be washed.

"I been there, done that with pristine this and pristine that and everything is perfectly in order. Where you had to wear the right kind of tie, the right kind of shoes, you've got the right kind of car and the right kind of everything. That's like having a leash on myself.

"After I moved into the boarding house, the state had me go through a course of sex offender treatment or SOT. I don't know how many weeks I went there. The doctor who wrote the course proudly stated that he had worked up the sex offender treatment manuals for about one third of the counties in the state. I filled out the papers we had to fill out, dotted i's and crossed t's, and he graduated me from the course, but nothing of what he said applied. Nothing. When you're diagnosed with 'latent deviant sexual desires on your grandmother's side' or whatever the hell in the family, it is not contributing to the solution, it's just more wordiness to this opaque shield that you really can't understand. Emotions rule us. The impact of emotions on people worldwide can be seen through all of history, and there was never a word about that.

"I don't care what your IQ is, there are people in decent families who turn out to be fairly inhuman, and there are people in inhuman families that turn out to be great. The difference is our individual ability to process our emotions and then grow spiritually.

"One of the 12 Steps is an amends step, and involved in that is understanding that I'm not responsible for what other people do, but I am responsible for what I have caused others to do. If I get angry at you about something, and I throw a brick through your window, I not only need to apologize, but I need to repair the window.

"A year or two after my release, I was attending the local drug court to be supportive of the recovering people in it. Of course, Judge W. was there and so was the DA I knew. Judge W. had been the presiding judge at my trial, and he went further than he had to, because he knew I was lying. He was angry at me. As for the prosecuting attorney who later became the district attorney, I had caused him a lot of stress. I realize he did some things that he should not have done that would qualify in my world as a sin. I realized that if I had not done the crime I did and acted as I had during the trial, he would not have done his actions, so I bear a certain responsibility.

"It gradually grew on me that they are responsible for their own anger, but if I fostered that or I enabled it, I played a part in some way, shape, or form. If I participated in it, I needed to address my role and stop minimizing, qualifying and avoiding. So I made an appointment with the DA and I apologized to him. I made amends. He said, 'Sam, I'm not mad at you. We're not mad at you. We know that you've changed.' He was very loving and very supportive, but I was the one who needed to say that to him, to clear that debt.

"I also made an appointment to meet with the judge. His guard dog secretary was right there behind him, ready to jump into the fray, because she didn't know if I was going to attack him or what. Most people he's dealt with had a lot of anger. I apologized to him for the part I played. I didn't say that I caused him to sin, however, I apologized for not being forthright. I didn't try to explain why, I said I just needed to apologize, and if I hadn't done that, it would still be a burden on me today. He was very gentle. I don't think he ever had anybody say that to him before. It was a cleansing on my part, because during the trial I could see he was disgusted with me; I was guilty as hell and I was just wasting taxpayers' money and his time.

"He and the DA were both extremely civil, there was no haughtiness or rubbing my nose in it. It was very peaceful in both cases. I don't believe for a minute they'd ever had people like me apologize. It was not a matter of courage on my part, it was just necessary, like the revelation you can't drink anymore—I need to do this or never be well. I am slow to recognize the damage I do to other people, but I do it to my soul first. I am terrified that my ex-wife or stepdaughter would want to see me. I couldn't live through that, but I try to clean up what I can from the past.

"The DOC, of course, doesn't trust you, so about three or four months after I got out, I went for a mandatory lie detector test. They want to see if I've been sneaking out at night, or emailing young girls or what have you. On a polygraph test you know the questions in advance that they're going to ask you and what your answer should be. They ask you three questions in three sets; if your answer is the same each time, then you're not lying, but if there's a bump, then there's an issue.

"The first time I did the polygraph, no problem. The second time I'm practicing rigorous honesty and a new way of living. The second question on the second set triggered me. It was, 'Have you ever committed a crime that you haven't told anybody about?' Suddenly I remembered when I worked for a convenience store company that had been abusing my wife in terms of finances and hours and everything else. I got pissed off and ripped them off for $60 worth of merchandise. On previous tests, I'd answered no, but this time I said yes, and man oh man, now I've done it. I screwed up the polygraph test and I don't know if I'm going back to prison. It was the longest, most miserable ride I'd ever had in my life, that trip with my PO (probation officer), but I was learning how to be rigorously honest, and that day was a significant day for me.

"They handed me a telephone. I could call the fire department, sheriff's department, police department, hospital, 911, my PO. I called one human being, my friend Billy; he was in recovery with me, and everyone else was authorities. I dialed Billy's number, and he answered the phone and said, 'Sam, how're you doing?' and I said, 'Billy, I'm angry and I'm afraid.' That was the first time in my life I'd ever been simply, openly and directly honest with another human being. What a new adventure.

"Then I explained to my PO what happened. That time it didn't have negative consequences, and I passed the next test fine. The point is I reached out to someone with intimate accuracy. I admitted my emotions, and Billy and others in recovery enable that."

Sam was learning to keep it — everything

in his life — simple and straightforward, an integral part of recovery. As he learned what a difference candor can make, he also found more friends, and at this point they were genuine friends. Perhaps they were the brothers in arms he had longed for during his Vietnam years when he wanted so badly to belong somewhere. These friends, however, were on a completely different path, that of recovery.

Tony was another one who befriended Sam through 12 Step meetings, "where I was just another suffering crook" Sam said. "He instantly knew I needed somebody in my life. He was very loving to me and his wife tolerated me. He was always a beautifully dressed human being: perfectly coiffured, polished shoes, a crease in the pants. Tony didn't like to drive in the city, so I'd drive him to meetings, appointments here and there, and we'd hang out together. I'd take him to his medical appointments and his car appointments, and he loved to go to delicatessens if they had real

Italian food. We were buds.

"It takes courage to befriend me, because most of these people have family or friends, and what are they going to think? Somebody like me, ex-convict, three times divorced, child molester, on and on, but they dared to befriend me. In recovery, what matters is who you are now and who you want to be rather than what you were. I've got guys in prison that I love. They'll never get out, but for me what matters is who they are now, the kind of person they've become, not what they did.

"One Sunday morning about a year after I moved into the boarding house, the front door opens, and in comes this stranger carrying a box. He's on the church council, and he'd announced at the council meeting that morning he had some homemade bread and after the meeting, he planned to take it to the boarding house. He and his wife dared enough to care, to get outside the bounds of the pews and the door, and à la Christ, to go where the sinners are. He and his wife and I would sit in my room and talk. Eventually I got invited to go to their church. I knew I would blow it off. I didn't want to tell him the truth, because I believed only those two would welcome me over there. I have a new sensitivity now that other people may feel uncomfortable around me.

"I believed that if I started going, sooner or later somebody's going to come up to me and say 'we really appreciate you being here and hope you're getting something from it, but don't you think you ought to start thinking as we do?' Any preacher with a fire in his belly would be saying 'we love you, we love you, we love you. Oh, by the way, shouldn't you start believing as we do and maybe do confirmation?'

"Perhaps this is a misplaced fear. I understand the psychology behind religion, that you get to participate and be a member of something, and I believe Christ is real, but I don't trust all the -isms that have been created in his name."

Throughout our talks Sam would gesture down the road toward the nearby new church, where he was sure he would be asked for a donation if he showed up. His money would be welcome, but he doubted he would be. He disagreed with their conservative theology anyway, he said, because it seemed to exclude people.

Sam had lived at the rooming house for year and a half when about 11 p.m. one night he heard noises. When he looked down the hallway, the resident manager and his girl-friend were hauling things out of their room. At about midnight the manager knocked on Sam's door and said, 'Here, take the keys. I'm leaving.' The following day the owner told Sam 'You've been here awhile, you might as well be the manager now.' The new responsibility and the aspect of power it brought with it would test Sam's primary resolution to treat everyone with kindness.

"I've been a self-centered jerk as a person," Sam said, "but I was always a good manager. I've always had a good eye for organization. This is how it should be: you don't put the green beans over by the laundry soap. I cleaned that place, I scrubbed and got things organized. It wasn't like running a Fortune 500 company, but there was still a lot to do after 30 years of zero upkeep except emergency repairs and nobody to do it but me. I busted my butt, and the owner saw the benefits and appreciated it.

"In many ways I've been just as deadly to the soul with my mouth in demeaning someone as I have been in other ways. For a few years there at the boarding house, I started heading back in the direction of anger and domination, justification and rationalization. So as manager, if I saw your window open at 1:00 a.m. in January or you were blasting the radio in your room at 3:00 a.m. in the morning, I would go up and pound on the door, and I was not very gentle — I'd let you know what kind of stupid son of a bitch you are through the tone of my voice, if nothing else.

"It took me four to five years to realize that behavior was not loving and I need to start moderating what I do. I had felt rage and hate, and I had felt less than others, so I put others down to make myself feel better. I started watching my attitude and therefore watching my mouth. Not everybody responded to that well but others did, so I was creating fewer enemies. I started leaving fewer scarred souls. Later on, I met a few people who told me, 'Oh, yeah, glad to know you, glad you were there.' So something positive does happen. It was a fabulous learning experience for me, ultimately.

"As I started feeling better, I started feeling less remorse, guilt and shame. I wished I hadn't said some things I said to others because I recognized I wouldn't like to be spoken to like that. That's part of recovery programs, to pass on to others what you want for yourself.

"Around town, I guess I was locally fa-

mous— I don't know another word to use —
in terms of lecturing, and a lot of people asked
me to sponsor them in my 12 Step groups. Un-
fortunately, I didn't know how to be a sponsor, and every damn one of them, as most do,
went back out and started drinking again.
The first couple of years when I had sponsees, I thought, 'I'm going to fix them sons of
bitches!' So at 1:00 am in the morning, I'd be
up reading every recovery book I could find,
looking for that phrase, that paragraph, that
word that would reach them and save them.

"I had the recovery books and literature
that I underlined and highlighted in different
colors. I still wanted to control, to fix, direct
and micromanage everything in between. I
was in a state of no trust, no God, no faith,
no nothing. I was back in charge again and I
would make the difference.

"One night, sitting at my desk, I realized my
fixing things was not for the other person. I
wanted to control them so my life wasn't hectic

or disrupted. It finally dawned on me, do your part and shut up. It's their journey, and I'm just part of it. It was part of my growth to 'Let go and let God.' I can care about this person, but I can't fix them. I can't help them, and I can't change them. And that's service: doing your part and leaving the rest.

"I also wrote letters and even kept copies of some. The letters are just me spouting off to somebody, lecturing somebody or being nice to somebody... explaining, explaining, explaining instead of just loving them and caring about them. The letters are a good reminder for me to sit down and shut up. It's all been written already anyway; recovery books are full of these stories. God's got it and I don't, and it took me a few three-ring binders to learn that.

"Then there was a guy named Bob in Room One, one of the most fundamentally deceitful and dishonest people I've ever met in my life. He was secretive about it, too. The owner was the same way, and these two were buds. The owner would tell me, 'you've got to tighten up here, do this, do that.' I would do this and that, then two months later he'd come back, and he'd let Bob do whatever he wanted and disrupt everything I had just put in order.

"One day, a corroded pipe in the basement bathroom burst, and the owner berated me in front of Bob and four other tenants. He got after me in a hateful way that showed he was halfway to full dementia. He told me to quit picking on Bob, and he was going to physically assault me. I felt a murderous rage, I was that angry. It took me a couple days to let go. I did that with other people by talking in meetings about how hurt and angry I was, and by sharing my feelings of betrayal. If the owner of the boarding house, his partner and Bob from Room One showed up at my door today, I would still feel anger. I'm not dead or completely I'm not healed yet, but I'm going in the right direction. There is still room to grow.

"During the 11 years I was at the boarding

house, it offered a lot of challenges. Overall, though, I did a good job there and I was getting better."

Before and after some of my visits with him, I roved the constricted landscape of Sam's current life, the corner gas station where he posts his torrent of letters, the church down the hill beyond town, the short main street with the requisite strip mall, courthouse and maple trees. There are places he doesn't allow himself to go in this town for fear of relapse or of traumatizing those he has hurt. He has put the few tired, near-windowless bars and the county fairgrounds off limits, and he goes to no classic car shows, no county fairs.

My tours included passing the boarding house, an off-white two story older home expanded with several unremarkable angular additions. I was seeing the exterior of Sam's suffering and growth, I realized. He was revealing to me the far more interesting invisible geography and the textured interior of recovery.

Lost Man Found

THIRTEEN

Letting Go of the World

The stress of life in the boarding house, the tenants, and the owner created a real need for Sam to move after that incident with the busted pipe. He had given it his best effort, and although the many structural problems were solvable, he learned that the social and spiritual problems there were beyond his control.

Sam had to get out and, in December 2016, he bought a home for the first time in his life. The house had been carved up with plywood into three rental units and needed work.

Thanks to smoking, he no longer had great health, but he had time, some money, and now, for the first time, friends.

"With the help of recovery friends, we restored it," he said. "One crew took out a four by eight section of the kitchen wall, which made a dramatic difference, while others worked on the basement and garage. I found sofa pillows, bought bookshelves, and potted plants including an hibiscus, which I killed by overwatering.

"Priority number one is not the house, however, it's people who stop in. We can speak intimately about who and what we were, like in a 12 Step meeting. It's not the typical football or job talk here, what we talk about is what's going on with us.

"A friend arrived with a rocker and an old floor lamp, and four hours later, we've emptied two coffee pots and filled an ash tray. My sponsor and I sat for an hour one night, people have stopped for 10 or 15 minutes and as long as five hours, letters arrive from prisoners, the mother of a prisoner writes, never-met friends write.

"One of the things I've learned is less is more. I don't really need this place, and I think about a smaller house and maybe just a begging bowl for rice like a Buddhist monk — I understand now the value of that. This doesn't feel self-abusive, shall we say, more like a monk in a desert starving himself to make himself pleasing to God.

"Then it starts translating into the smaller things in daily living, like just saying thank you about the birds at my feeders.

"Every time I get worried because someone is not here yet or I light up a cigarette or I want to kill a squirrel in my birdfeeders, or I'm worried about this or worried about that, I'm still not very spiritual. I am still full of me; I'm not at third grade yet.

"I'm so full of me: I want my cigarettes, I want my chocolate, I want my lawn how I want my lawn. I've been frazzled the past three or four days about the shrubbery, and who are we going to get to move those rocks? I've also got to get the lattice on the porch up. Because of my health, I can't do it myself.

"One afternoon, I took a piece of paper and a cup of coffee and my ashtray and sat down, on the balcony, not a bird in sight, and I started worrying, did the orioles go south already? Then they started coming — red-breasted gross beaks, finches, woodpeckers and the orioles, and what a thrill. I just sat there and told myself sit down and shut up, let go and let God. Enjoy the moment instead of the 'I've got to do' lists, enjoy the greenery and that stream back there in the wall of forest.

"Now I just go out there and say thank you. If I get this done, if I get that done, or if I die first, so be it.

"People, places, and things are taking an increasingly second place in life, and you couldn't have explained that to me when I was 21 or 35. It's a sense that peace and serenity are somewhat available even in the midst of good stress and bad stress.

"I can't grow spiritually until I'm aware of my emotions, and now I'm aware, and that's where it starts. I identify with people now, I know exactly what they are talking about, and I see we are a band of brothers and sisters, all the same, although we may do the same exact thing in different ways.

"I am aware I have tons of friends around here now, but I don't bowl, fish, hunt, or get invited to family social occasions. Friends will stop and visit if they are working on a chicken coop or fixing a truck motor a few miles from here, but I don't push. I turned that over a long time ago to spiritually let others make the decision about what kind of relationship, if any, they want to have with me. Some people may wonder, well, how come Sam doesn't call and invite himself over? I have an inviolate rule: I make phone calls, but I'll be damned if I'm going to pick up the phone and call somebody just to chit chat, I will not do it.

"I am not going to be that odd uncle that always gets invited over for Christmas dinner. I'm not going to call people and say, 'Hey, what are you doing? I thought I'd come over and visit for a minute.' That's wrong. It'd be driven not by affection for the other person but by looking to satiate myself, and I'm just not going to go there except for chocolate and cigarettes.

"At times, the singleness becomes aloneness and is a bitter experience, but Christ himself sought aloneness at times. Now I think the distraction of the crowds at county fairs or a family gathered for any social event can blunt depth of connection.

"I have a different lifestyle now, purposely so, and it goes back to how quickly I can change. I don't feel like a powder keg, I don't feel psychotic, but if you give me a glass of beer, I'm probably going to start drinking. If I quit smoking and you give me a cigarette, I'm probably going to start again.

"Slow and slower is not all bad. Puttering along at less than the posted mph is intentional, and I avoid cities so as to not get sucked into the have to/gotta. I did not live an insightful life, was not aware, nor willing to be. I am now and desire to foster that. Letters and chats with others foster that.

"I have an established set of principles that have been hard won by letting go of people, places, and things. It was in one of the books I read when I was locked up or maybe after I got out, how, each morning, Buddhist monks take their bowls and go from house to house for food. They don't really beg, because everybody knows what they are doing. What they are doing is submitting.

"Instead of going out and buying a bag of Snickers and T-bone steaks and sitting back on a lawn chair, these people live non-materialistically. Maybe a rice farmer did all the work growing and collecting the rice and doesn't have much to eat himself, but he gives them a little bit. And that's called participating in life and taking what comes.

"I take my inventory daily: I don't do it all day long, but my triggers are the seven deadly sins of Pride, Anger, Greed, Gluttony, Lust, Envy, and Sloth — I call them the PAGGLES. I keep a notebook – 'my inventory' – of 40,000 pages of newspaper clips where I recognize PAGGLES. As soon as I experience any of those in any degree, I'm exhibiting fear, not love, and need to back up and reassess. It's like being a diabetic and saying the hell with it, I'm going to eat a 32-ounce Hershey's candy bar. Maybe you shouldn't take that first bite out of the corner.

"The PAGGLES seem benign, but some are deadly. The very first two sins I take on are pride, which means I set myself apart, and sloth, which is I'm not going to take care of it now, maybe tomorrow, or I will do that later, or you need to go first.

"I'm more quiet about my pride, and I'm

trying to manage my anger, and I'm not going to punch you in the mouth when I am angry. When I get prideful about something or angry about something, I get angry at myself, and I fight against them now (except cigarettes).

"I had a housemate, a young guy who was in prison and did a 180, the same as me, and I got to watch the miracle unfold. I would be disappointed if he had started hauling in women and drugs and so forth, but I wouldn't hate him, whereas 10 years ago I would have.

"I don't keep notes on books any longer, and I don't read books much anymore, to tell the truth. I don't make the time for it, partly because of all the recovery meetings I go to — six a week. God and those people around the table at those meetings have raised me. Of myself, I am nothing. I was sitting there at a meeting recently on the verge of tears, because that group, and especially the five or six who have been there longest, they're my family.

"I'm here to grow my soul, not lose myself

in people, places, and things. This is a choice, but it's not an easy one all the time. This is personified by several examples, the first one that leaps to mind are monks living in self-imposed exile in cells, spending their time in prayer and meditation. I am letting go of the world and putting it in its proper perspective.

"In Mother Theresa's journals after she died, they found a lot of angst, but she got up every damn morning and let go of the world. That same leper she had fed, doctored, and clothed three or four times before was back again, and she cared for him. That's letting go of the world.

"I feel incredibly blessed, but it's been real hard to put that into action sometimes by saying there will be no violence."

FOURTEEN

Paying It Forward

One of the blessings that allows Sam to live in his own home, on his own schedule, and to pursue recovery largely full time is that he is retired. He can live this way because of several unique circumstances.

"When I was at the private prison up north, I got a letter from an attorney that my dad had died and left money to me and my sister," he explained. "I would put myself to bed at night wondering what I could do in a proactive way with that money, trying to calculate how much interest it would be generating. I figured it wasn't going to be much for the first few years, but I knew it would build, and my plan was to just put it away. Then in 2016, there was more money, a lot more. Dad had sold a thriving business, and his second wife after Mom died had also passed away. She owned a farm, had a teacher's pension, and in addition to the house, they had a cabin. At one time, Dad even had a plane. When I told my PO, she said 'Sam, it looks like you're a millionaire!'

"To me, the issue is not what I have, but how quickly I could get rid of it. My primary intent was to live minimally and protect the funds far into the future for the benefit of others less fortunate. With help, I was able to set up a long term charitable trust that centers on donating to the causes I care about. I was determined to not let the money change me, but instead, give me a chance to make a difference for others.

"I try to give small amounts in a measured

way. At the cash register I can give $5 or $10 for the little old lady behind me in the checkout line. When a friend's son died, I took a card to my 12 Step meeting, we all signed it, and I put $50 in it for gas money. I fund an American Legion scholarship every year, and with the local church, I send them $25 a month, anonymously.

"One day, I went to our VA service office and said 'You must have vets come in here who are hard up.' The staff said, 'Yes, there are some, but the VA has limited resources.' So I bought $50 gas cards and gave them anonymously to the VA to be used for vets in need. In my world this is a way to practice humility; it keeps me off the front page of my own mind.

"People come into your life for a season, reason or lifetime. I once met a woman who was one angry, hostile, defensive, go-it-alone human being. Now we are loving friends who have grown together and can speak intimately about what the hell is going on. She is dirt poor and always has been. I send her $50 a week, and she puts it to good use raising her grandson.

"Little things like these make sense to me. I seek ways that are non-mega, things that are meaningful in a hands-on way, things that are relational, rather than sending a check to the American Cancer Society or something. I want to be more personal, so I like digging into my kitty and giving something a friend needs without a note or letter or shaking hands.

"Five or six years ago I started actively growing an empathetic conscience. I now know what it means to care, to be honorable. I now feel for people, and I have even dared to consider my many victims in many ways. I can actually envision what those men I killed in Vietnam must have felt like. I can now imagine the mother and father of the young man I killed when I was drinking and driving must have felt like at his funeral. I can now imagine what my stepdaughter must have felt like. I can now imagine the horrible emptiness of what Julie lived all of her life.

"I now feel for people and I shed tears. I cry now because I know what was what I was not; what so many were. Same way with Lucy — I know what she was and I was not, and I cry sincere tears for what I was not able to be. I really do care about her and Teddy. I will never live long enough to make amends for who and what I was when I knew them. Nobody stands out as much as Lucy. I never pressed for information on her, but I hear she went on to get married, has a job and children. I'd like to anonymously help her in some way, but I think the best thing I can do is to stay out of her life. If she or Patsy, my first wife, showed up at my door, I'd have a heart attack and die; whether they hated or forgave me, I could not stand the pain. They are the two people I cannot face. That will take the loving embrace of a higher power.

"After I got out of prison, Teddy called me

a few times. It was difficult and I didn't know how to relate to him for the 15 minutes of those calls. It was shallow small talk, how he has a girlfriend and a new computer, a new Facebook page, etc. It was meaningless, but that's all he had. I felt so sad for him. I appreciated that he reached out to me, but he didn't know me and I didn't know him. It was all he knew of me — people, places and things. He didn't know my heart or who I really am inside.

"I've learned just as many things from the positive stuff, a lot of that in hindsight: now I see how my father didn't know how to show affection, but he did care. Now I know what a wonderful woman Patsy was. Now I recognize not too many lives then were *Father Knows Best*, most families were just winging it the best they could. My parents were not evil people, just human beings getting through life, trying to do what they thought was right. You could not have explained these things to me at that time. My shame came from knowing I'd drink the whole glass of water when you are dying of thirst. I was that indifferent to the needs of anyone but myself.

"When I got out, I craved 12 Step recovery, because I knew my salvation and growth lay in the utter simplicity of the program. There's some important things in life to remember, and through 12 Steps, I have started remembering. I remember what a wonderful person Lucy was, so I do what little I can to not give her bad memories by staying out of her life, by avoiding places I might encounter her. I am more sensitive than I used to be, more thoughtful. I go to a 12 Step meeting every Sunday night. One night I'm reading Step Two: '…came to believe a power greater than ourselves could restore us to sanity.' Oh yeah, I understand insanity. I say this in meetings, and I tell my sponsees: I know I was crazy. It was insanity what I did. What I hear in stories from other people recovering is also insane. The founder of 12 Steps, Bill W., had a pipeline to God. I've started seeing how he wrote, the methodology to it, and he wasn't talking about insanity. He mentions the word 'faith' 23 times in step four of the 12 steps. Faith means the virtues, no matter what, and it's faith in a power greater than ourselves that matters.

"No matter what, I have to respond in a virtuous way. Gandhi, Mother Theresa, Christ, and Dr. King all operated on, 'I will not respond in violence no matter what you do to me.' I am trying to do the same. So I'm not going to take a knife and stab that boarding house owner, and I cannot justify cursing him, putting salt in his sugar or anything. I don't have to speak to him, but I need to be civil even if I don't want to."

Whenever Sam and I talk, I ask him about his health — it is usually poor although he doesn't complain. His mustache hides it, so at first I didn't notice that he is missing many teeth. He is so afraid of needles, he tells me, that he pulled nine of his own teeth in prison rather than have the prison dentist do it. I also ask whether he is sleeping. His answer is never positive, although he manages to make good use of his long waking hours.

"I don't sleep well, although I never did have nightmares, not even in Vietnam," he tells me. "When I wake up in the morning now, full of regret, it usually has to do with my personal habits in terms of hacking and coughing or, damn it, I've got to get to the bathroom. It's rarely got to do with anybody else anymore. So I spend fair amount of time awake at night, listening to radio programs. In the quietness, when you are not inundated with people, places, and things, suddenly there's a freedom for new concepts, new evaluations of things in ways you never heard before."

Between visits over the months, Sam and I have become pen pals, with Sam's contribution to the exchange surpassing mine by at least ten to one. His envelopes, persistently addressed to "Mrs. Karin Winegar" (I am Ms and have told him so), are often adorned with holiday stickers or a return address label from one of the charities he supports. He mails me book reviews, pounds of pages of adages and sheet after sheet of Irish humor.

He encloses an article about the 1971 Stanford Prison Experiment (a study of power using student volunteers cast as prisoners and guards), feature stories on generous athletes and mystery philanthropists, a juicy essay on the nature of truth by Yuval Noah Harari in the *Bloomberg View*, and inexplicably, an article about the Hitchcock film *Rebecca* from *Country Life* magazine. I arranged for him to receive copies of the sermons from my progressive Congregational church. He calls them "powerful lessons each time in humility and how far I have yet to travel." He addresses his letters "Zowie!" or "Good Morning" and concludes them with "More Will Be Revealed " or "Thanks for Being Part of My Life."

One day a bright orange greeting card

adorned with a photo of a basket of snoozing puppies arrives. It is not signed. Inside is a letter penned in his trademark capitals "…ran across some things about midnight which flowed into 4 a.m. this morning all because I ran across a blank puppy card. And the epiphany moments came non-stop… I can and do weep with regret and sorrow—good. As opposed to never. My heart and soul were diseased. Have scars now but they are proof positive of having met my demons. Actively fought and not lost …Peace is available."

On the margin of a newspaper clipping slipped into the card he has added "Love is a verb. Be. Do. Act."

Perhaps peace is available to him, but for Sam, rest is rare and always has been.

"There are hours when I'm awake and don't listen to the radio, too," he writes in another letter. "Who can dare face the insignificance of 3:30 a.m.? Blunted by the whir of a fan only. No radio, no TV, no CD to shield the psyche. No purpose. None. Just be. No book, crossword, Sudoku, meditational, list of 'to do's' — who dares sit in profound silence letting time pass? 'Tis not idle time, nor meditation, nor planned. 'Tis wholly new, even scary or sobering. Sixty plus years of get, do, be, achieve, plan, accomplish are really, truly without meaning."

He lives a largely tech-free life — no TV — and the flip side of the loneliness and insomnia, he writes me, is "not all bad. Old time radio shows on for an hour or so. With no boob tube, must do some imagineering (Disney term). There is no 'now' commanding (me) for repeated news and sports. (My) brain is not locked into the immediate and so insight thrives unfettered by repeated humdrum. In detachment, there is wonderful expansion."

The contemplative prisoner-monk role may be his ideal. Above all, he says, "I don't want to be phony. I don't want to be dishonest any more. I recognize now that if I really want to change, I have to do it spiritually.

"Empowerment in my past was just not giving a crap," he adds. "I wanted to feel! I used sex, TV, chocolate, money, drinking, anything in trying to feel. They didn't work. It's turned into I don't care what other people think — in a healthy way. Now I see the one-ness, not our differences.

"I'm not going to start distorting and bending the core me, because I never knew a core me, and now I do.

"This stuff that I spout and all these revelations are not unique to me, it's a gift from God and good people. After a life of creating pain and destruction, I have been given much. I want to make sure I use what I've been given to bring about good."

Those Inside, Those Outside

Most murderers are not born, they are created — that's what Sam tells me. As he recovers, he sees how the sensitive boy, "hung out to dry," as he describes it, was on his way to being emotionally diseased and spiritually dead.

In part, functionality and indifference were part of the parenting style of the post-war times, he speculates. Whatever the reason, no one noticed, no one got close to him, and quite soon it was too late. In his exclusion from intimacy and protection, he became one of the men on the inside of prisons and the outside of love. Now, as he experiences love and acceptance, he understands that he had to be distant from emotion in order to protect himself.

"Feeling and caring gets you nothing but hurt by the people you trust and respect the most," he says. "It was absolutely life and death for me. So I've never in my life been close to anybody. For a long time, I thought I had been close, but I really didn't know how to be. I would have a spark of those feelings of intimacy and connection. I really did care about my first wife. I really did care about my first girlfriend. I really did care about some of the guys in 'Nam. It is like I know how to sit behind the wheel of a car and start it up, but I don't know how to drive. Same thing. I didn't have the skills to authentically connect with another human being.

"Those of us off the deep end are effectively alone. The only thing I can do to survive is to remain that way, detached from feeling, and therefore no human being is safe from me. Addicts, alcoholics, prisoners — we can't deal with pain.

"Most psychobabble dances around these issues. In SOT (Sex Offenders Training), all they did was rub my nose in what I did, just like my mom and dad had. When it's always punishment and consequences, then I avoid, lie, twist, distort, forget, and rationalize. I do not go to a root cause, because I don't know how. Instead I find a way to cope by medicating myself.

"Now, in all my news clippings, I see human behavior over and over and over — it goes to root causes. The simplicity of the 12 Step program is a godsend, because it addresses those root causes. How alone I was is not unique to me. Those who sit in prison, they don't see it and guards don't, either. So you're detaching, detaching, detaching, and if you're not attached to something, you don't float free, you sink. It's a horrible way to feel, because it's like eating food that has no nutritional value; you're doomed to starve and die. You want to live, you want to feel good, but you don't know how, and the horrible part is you're alone. Even if you knew what the hell to talk about, you don't have anybody to talk to.

"Most guys in prison are gonna get out exactly the same as when they went in. Usually when you're inside, it's 'you and I be bros forever, don't forget me' — that crap, that artificially manufactured connection. But the minute you walk out the damn prison door you forget it. The average inmate is thinking about the sex, booze, money, drugs and TV they will have when they get out. And I call the DOC the Department of Confinement, not Corrections, because that's about all they do.

"It's not intelligence but emotions that drive us, and they do it most dramatically like the bombers or mass shooters, like some of our politicians. The men who commit massacres like those in Texas, Las Vegas, Florida, wherever — it starts with 'I matter, and I will show you.' We have an impenetrable shell around us to protect the 'I'. There are a few people in 12 Step programs or Pope Francis who don't need it maybe, but most of us are on that journey at different points.

"Now I'm not alone anymore, and I'm just ecstatic about that. I don't have all the usual social situations; however, I've been with the people in 12 Step meetings, and they're my family. One blade of grass does not make a lawn, all of them do. People in 12 Steps are all affiliated, we can sit and talk intimately, and I can say anything. We communicate with, not at one another, and that is a great gift. It's a pie in the sky wish, but I wish the world could speak like that. We are not locked into talking about drunkenness or recovery, either, so it frees me up to see the whole human being. I fall in love with who they are instead of what they are and what they look like, and I know love for the very first time, and that's sweet.

That is the greatest gift of all. I've been a wannabe all my life, and I thought that life meant going here or doing this, owning this, owning that. I never knew how to be with somebody. I don't fault anybody for that anymore.

"Every -ist I ever had is still available, like being sexist or racist. But I find value now in letting them go. If I come home and somebody's broken a window, I'm going to be upset, but nothing like in the past. Some situations are more difficult than others, but all of them are easier now. I look at myself as a monk here, but not a very good monk. I am a cheating monk, because rather than really getting spiritual, I am still doing the cigarettes and eating the cookies. I'm angry at myself and ashamed because of the smoking. I'm still full of wants. And don't ask me to start walking to town rather than driving my truck, even in nice weather.

"What's really important — and *The Last Samurai* movie exemplified that — is honor, respect, dignity, integrity and keeping your word. Over the years in prison, I fantasized about somehow being able to get transferred to an abbey where I could just bake bread, hide, and be productive at the same time instead of facing the world. I wanted it for the wrong reasons. Now I know who I am, appreciate that and the growth that my higher power and good people have fostered in me, yet the result of my life has been nothing I ever wished for in terms of worldliness, spouse, children, steady job, good friends to chum around with, and so forth.

"I've come home again, like a full circle, to when I was 11, 12, or 13 years old by myself with effectively no mom or dad. Instead of building ship and plane models or reading novels alone up in my room, however, I'm doing more positive things. I also go into the forest now to appreciate the silence and the trees rather than to cut them down and sell them for wood to make money. I have a deeper sense of appreciation of this world. I got out of prison knowing what not to do, but I didn't know how to live. I've learned that in recovery. To learn how to live you've got to interact with other people, and you have to choose.

"Now that I have a conscience, I'm gentler and more considerate with others. If you show up with a purple Mohawk hairdo and ask me, "Is this attractive?' I'll say 'it's not too bad...' knowing it could be worse.

"This sounds horribly egotistical, but I can identify now with God, Mother Theresa, and Christ. I don't think Christ felt too darn bad about leaving this planet. He was here as a man, he felt, he cared, but I don't know how that poor guy put up with it as long as he did. I believe it's accurately reported that on the cross he said, 'Father, forgive them, for they know not what they do.' At first, I thought he meant the Jews and Romans that were killing him. Now what I believe he meant was the entirety of humanity past, present and future.

"In *The Green Mile*, Big John is on death row, and although he's innocent, he's going to be executed. He turns to the warden named Paul and says 'The needles in my head, I can't stand it anymore. You'd be doing me a favor.' Big John could feel the pain of everyone, he felt it for humanity. Now I feel it for myself and humanity.

"Thirty years ago, I felt hostile when somebody mentioned the word God, because to me it was only holy-rolling-mumbo-jumbo clap-trap. I was raised Catholic, which taught 'God loves you, God loves you, God loves you,' but it also seemed to say 'here's all the ways you're wrong, all the ways you're sinful and you can't be redeemed.' When I saw the word 'God' in the recovery books, it was a challenge, but I went on.

"When I started reading 12 Step books, I read them with prejudice, looking for errors. I want nothing that will allow me to take a detour again. The detours I've taken have been deadly to myself and other people. People are still more religious than spiritual (which I believe is true for most of the world), so I shy away from trying to explain the differences in that to them if they are not there yet. They will see what I do with my life in a physical and material way. They will judge me on my behavior not on the redemption God creates in my life. If you have a long history of being a dedicated religious person, I want to be helpful, but I don't want to be challenging. If you are not part of nor willing to be part of an organized structure, that is a threat to most organized religious organizations. To change you have to be willing to grow, to expand your way of thinking and perceiving things. Usually that doesn't happen instantly, we have to work at it."

One morning, while the coffee steamed and grew cold in our cups, as the tiny tape recorder ran on and I listened to Sam, I recalled how my father used the expressions of his day. One of them was "get religion" as in, "when he heard that diagnosis, he really got religion."

As Sam's story unrolled over the months, it was clear Sam did not "get religion" in prison or ever. What he got, by both of our definitions, was a growing understanding of human behavior, the ability to let go of his will to control things and people. He gained a devotion to his own spiritual well-being. He began to live and listen more inwardly, to act and react less selfishly, and to love more authentically.

"The most fearsome choice I ever made was to step away purposely and with forethought from the religion of my youth," he told me. "Since the first time Dad or Mom carries you to church, it is doom and gloom, hellfire and damnation if you don't go along. I had to make a decision and either keep one foot in religion to look good and get along or I could dare to do something different."

As I listened to Sam I thought about what a prominent lawyer once told me about how

many prisoners seem to have a religious con-
version in jail. How it can be the default position of the terrified, traumatized or cunning.
With Sam, it was none of that. It was genuine.

Meeting My Maker

Sam's reliance on a higher power is not dogmatic or unquestioning. It is vibrant, discerning, and deep, and he puts it into practice daily. His awareness is the byproduct of years of lonely thought, ongoing study, emotional struggle, and paying attention to life. This lost man became found not in a lightning strike of illumination but over years of asking himself what matters and requesting divine guidance. I am convinced he got it, not in a passionate theological sense but in something more gritty, more earthbound and ultimately much more human.

"Who I am becoming and the evil I left behind is part of my story; but the essence of the story is how I manage to do that," he says to me. "If you tell a kid to saddle a horse but they've never done it before, how do they know what to do? Now I am attached to my spiritual purpose. It's not complete, it's not welded, but now that I have a conscience and a sense of purpose, I can't go backward, not and live with myself.

"Miraculous things happened to me, and I now believe I've been kept alive for a reason. I didn't have any awareness of why I've been protected, but now all these incidents have started to make sense to me."

There is one more incident Sam related to me that I found provocative. "In the fall of 1965, I personally chased and caught up to a UFO, an honest-to-God real one," he said, early on in our work together. "I got out of my dad's Rambler station wagon, leaned over the roof and stood there for a minute to two minutes and watched this thing holding. It was an exceptionally clear late afternoon and no mistaking what I saw. It was the shape of a child's top with a lot of windows, and it moved at tremendous speed at right angles. I don't think of that often, but I know that we are not alone in this universe, and maybe humans are not the best that God could do. I believe spiritual beings guide us and offer us chances.

"Here at the tail end of my life, I have some hopeful goodness and a profound sense of my journey, which I believe was of my higher power. In Vietnam, so many guys were traumatized, wounded and so many died in terrible battles. I didn't. I was 19 and stupid. And I was lucky. God kept me alive for a purpose and long enough to know the truth.

"I tell my sponsees that when I die and meet my maker, there's only going to be one question on the table: What did you do to grow your soul spiritually? Not who did you kill, who did you molest, how much money did you drop in the basket on Sunday morning or what is your opinion in politics? The main question is what we do to grow our soul spiritually?

"The truth is, our sole purpose for existence is enlightenment. All conflict arises from pursuit of empowerment instead.

"Does it get more simple than that? I think not. For a person to see like this, they need to be willing to call into question everything they currently have, and that's a process. If I don't want to do the sweat equity or work of facing myself, then I can go to church, come home, have dinner and watch football—I can just dull myself to anything beyond the superficial. Earthquake, rape, a best friend murdered — we spend 24/7 working to never have to experience those things. Getting outside the box is not something human beings want to do. The box is the comfort zone, but there's no growth in the box. What does work — and I still feel uncomfortable saying it because it smacks of religion — is spirituality."

Here, when he sums things up, Sam sounds to me very much like Yoda, the monk-philosopher character in the *Star Wars* film series. It's not just his speaking cadence, which runs to the brief and declarative, but in his devotion to reducing things to their elements.

"There are only two choices: grow to be spiritual or do not grow," he tells me on many occasions. "You can respond emotionally to life or you can respond spiritually.

"Those are the only options. Acting spiritually is a virtue, and acting emotionally is corrupted emotion. We are so damn busy trying to be civilized that we don't know how to be spiritual. I am here to grow spiritually. Nothing on this earth is worth me damaging my soul. We are all alike, we are all the same — pink inside. The bottom line is we're biological entities, and we want to survive. I had to do anything to protect myself, so I enjoyed taking life when I was in Vietnam. I looked forward to it in the respect that it didn't bother me. I will do whatever I've got to do eventually to protect what I have. So you pull within, pull within if you don't have any resources without. There isn't any blame, that's just the way it is.

In that marathon writing session in prison, Sam concluded we are all controlled by fear. Over time, he tells me, he learned that salvation comes from transposing it into love and respect. We can think, speak, and act based in fear or love. Love does not diminish anyone emotionally.

"When I begin to believe there's more, I can start living with a less denigrating view of other people. I can see them as spiritual beings in transition same way I am. We need to find ways to peek inside ourselves and dare to get out of the status quo and the hope things will be different. We need to figure out a way to make them different.

"Love of humanity trumps everything else. It is supposed to. We are souls in a body, and we look at the body, but it's really the soul we deal with, and I have a responsibility to act in a way that's spiritually healthy toward that soul. We think we count when we have material things, but largely we don't know how to just get together, love, and share.

"Every day there's something appalling in the news. How do you move beyond that and grow? Our sole purpose is to grow spiritually. How do you motivate another person to do that or do it yourself?"

Sam's intense confessions to me over the months amplified my own interest in spiritual growth, but perhaps very few people meet or even want to meet a person like Sam. His insistence that salvation (spiritual, not religious) is available to everyone was a refrain in our conversations. His own path is 12 Step recovery, and he is ardent about the back of the 12 Step Big Book stories about "people who are gay, straight, males, females, fat, skinny, alcoholic and afflicted with every kind of craziness," he told me.

"Everyone's background is different, but we are all the same in one respect: we are emotionally driven. We are emotional creatures, and to progress, we have to learn how to grow spiritually and set emotions aside. Every person in the recovery stories found a spiritual path for enlightenment and acceptance, then acceptance leads to inner peace. Though we have different experiences, we are all on the same journey. I can identify with this other guy. All of us have been there, too. All the same church, different pew. Same experiences in a different way.

"I was not raised by bad, dumb, or evil people. I was raised by people who talked about politics, sex, football, and things of the world but not spirituality. They failed to teach the spiritual significance and eternal implication of things. They failed to put them in perspective. That can be very deadly. Look around at the world and consider what a few enlightened, spiritually connected people say and do compared with what everybody else says and does. Nothing I'm doing, going through, or recognizing is new or unique. It's new and unique to me, but this stuff's been going on for thousands of years. Our search for meaning is one we all share and because of that we can relate to each other.

"It helps, now, for me to realize I don't believe this is the only go around that we're going to have, and living each lifetime is an exercise in growing a soul. I've got to grow some spiritual muscle, and spiritual muscle means you're going to have to learn how to deal with things eventually. There's no time frame for that learning. A lot of the books I've read indicate that same thing. Loving does not have a schedule — you don't have to learn this by seventh grade.

"We grow by facing adversity, whether you're building a muscle or a brain or a soul. I have a long history of hiding out. At 12 Step meetings, I kept hammering at people about that damn seventh step: ask God to remove my shortcomings. How the hell does he do that? He does it by letting me live one more day and giving me the opportunity to choose a virtue over an emotion.

"Hopefully you will reach a perspective where you look at life through an eternal, spiritual lens instead of a well-rationalized emotional lens. You're going to come back in some lifetime to a spiritually-based way of looking at life rather than a well-rationalized emotional way. It's a scary journey to a lot of people, but it's actually total freedom.

"We armor ourselves with impersonal details about ourselves instead of exposing who we truly are. We share what we do, what we accomplish, what we know, what we own, where we've been and where we're going. And it doesn't work.

"We hide our vulnerability and ramp it up with more sex, more booze, more money, more clothes, then we either change or die miserably. We can learn that it's about who I am rather than what I've got, or how I look or anything else external.

"Tragedy happens whether you are a victim or victimizer — both can find love through spiritual principles. I know because I have been both. Tragedy, pain and heartache are part of life, and I learned more through being challenged and stressed by myself or by other people than by sitting alone in a field full of violets and lilies.

"Life is both agony and ecstasy, triumph and tragedy. We can ask what the purpose is of each and then put them in proper context. When I grow spiritually, keeping my purpose in mind, I can let go of the emotions I once turned into destructive vehicles. My path was one of desperation. I am still learning the discipline to continue on a better path.

"God don't make throwaway souls", Sam told me at almost every one of our meetings.

He also says you might as well do what you can to get it right this time so you've got less to deal with next time you come back.

"I do believe before we come back, we know what we are going to do and face. That the process is worked out between ourselves and our higher power. Tongue in cheek I tell my friends if God is mad at me, next time I come back he's going to make me a woman, because women have more to bear than men do.

"We submerge our anger and hate because we don't know how to cope. We rationalize the seven deadly sins and use them to cope with life. God created me for a purpose, and my purpose is to grow spiritually, to grow my soul. I cannot do that until I know the opposite. That was satiation, but that's all that was, temporary.

"Less is more in terms of worldliness," is one of Sam's cardinal rules now. "The example I like is Gandhi, who was born wealthy, he enjoyed sex, fine food, fine clothing. His wife actually had some resentments as he progressed spiritually, because he wasn't so much interested in those worldly things anymore. You could not have explained this to me when I was 18, but around 50 it was starting to come in. When I am worldly, I am dissatisfied with this and that. Now I have everything I always wanted, and I still deal with unhappiness, which is so very, very human. I don't need stuff to make me happy anymore."

Another of Sam's principles is that being of service gives us a place in this world. "That's why we were created, although we mostly fight that truth tooth and nail. It's around us every day all day worldwide through great spiritual leaders, and the examples they show us to submerge yourself to something better and a higher purpose.

"Mother Theresa experienced that. At night, oh, the tiredness and all the sorrow and the grief and the frustration. But every morning she got back up and took care of those people, some of them multiple returnees.

"The huge, fundamental change in my life since prison is in the expectations I have of other people. I can hope or want for them, but as soon as I have expectations, I am wrong and not seeing things as they really are. That's a mantra in my life. I'll share my candy bar with you, I'll help you mow your lawn, I'll give you a ride, but if I have expectations of how you will respond and grow based on my ideas about how you should, that is not service. The key is expectations. I can care about this person, but I can't fix them, I can't help them, I can't change them. And that's service, doing your part and leaving the rest.

"God gives all of us a 'bank account,' and the only thing to go into that bank account is love, unconditional love, and respect with immeasurable tolerance and patience. I can withdraw from that account at any time, but I also have to make deposits. So if I take out a dollar's worth, then I spend time with a dying friend, maybe 10 bucks goes in. If I take out a dollar's worth, and I wave at a friend as I'm driving by in the street, maybe a dime's worth goes in. We deplete that account by giving and doing with expectations, not with love. Then we feel bankrupt, and we are, because we're not living spiritually connected. I have expectations — selfishly.

"Life is about learning, it really is. We think it's about working, making money, accumulating, gathering, getting educated, degrees and acquiring and then retiring... every adjective and verb you can think of, but it's all about learning. It took me a long time to learn that. Sounds trite, but that's the way it is.

"God, or whatever your concept of a higher power is, wants us to have the exact same things that any loving parent would want. God created me not to be below him, he created me to be with him. He created my soul to be with him. He doesn't want to beat me, he doesn't want to shame me, but he has to let me go enough to experience the consequences of my choices. Then I can realize I don't want to do that particular thing anymore. Then, like any loving parent, be there for me with unconditional love and tolerance and patience unimaginable. It's like the story of the prodigal son — for each of us, God's going to love us enough to let us go and enough to welcome us back no matter where we've been and what we've done.

"I am older now and know profoundly that disfigurement of the psyche is a part of all living. No matter how untouched one may be by the darker aspects of living, disfigurement of the soul is a part of life. Reunification with our Creator means tiring of that state of being, then growing in humility. Probably not one in a million thinks introspectively; people are so busy with commuting and family and watching sports and doing dishes. And you gotta give up stuff, and nobody wants to do that. Who wants to drop their shoes and walk the way Christ did? Just a few of us sprinkled around on this earth that is school.

"I hope someone who reads this — though they may not have been to war, killed someone, or molested a child — can identify with this story in some way, shape, or form. Life for me has been all these experiences. I believe the only thing that's going to live beyond me is my soul, and this is just part of a decades-long or centuries-long process.

"I cannot converse with anyone about quantum mechanics and a great number of topics, but when it comes to life, living, why, how come, emotions, spirituality, etc., I have no doubt I can talk to anyone.

"I had no morals — capitalized, italics, underlined. Everything was about what I wanted or could take from someone. That was embedded in me as a child, and then when you take a human life, you have no restraint other than getting caught.

"I was lost. In that county jail I made a decision to turn my will and my life over to the care of a higher power. I feel like I've traveled a long way growing my soul, learning in difficult circumstances, getting tested. God let me live this long to find my way. When my time comes to finally leave this earth, I will be ready. I am so thankful."

Letter to the Men I Killed

18 July 1992

I don't know who you are. I know very little about you and even the little I do know is mostly an assumption and if you were to appear before me today, I would not know you by sight.

I believe you were young. I believe you were from what was called North Vietnam. We met in a small village or hamlet in South Vietnam on the Bong Song Plains, and I lived. You did not. I think there were two of you. The citation says there were seven of you and you were heavily armed with this and that. You were wounded and you wanted to live. The first of you did not, as I shot almost immediately. The second, afraid I am certain, fought to the death by dropping a grenade at my feet and you died. I did not.

I do not think of you daily. Not even each and every week, but I do think of you often. I wonder. I wonder about you. Your friends, your family. Your loved ones I wonder about everything I am curious and I will know little for certain.

As we cannot discuss events as old friends or comrades in arms would, I am left discussing things about you and about related items with myself. And, at times, those in my circle.

I have learned many, many things since my life. Since your deaths.

And, in truth, I sometimes seriously question who lived and who died, who went on and who stopped; 'suspect you know.

Yes. I have learned many things, and they

have all come at a price. Some have been very costly to myself and to others. Some of the lessons are still being taught, and perhaps always will be in this life. Others I have mastered quite quickly, and most are in the vast middle.

I have learned this.

I wish you were here. Now. At this moment. You are in my heart, but I wish you were here to touch, to smell, to hear. To clasp your hands in mine.

I believe you already know but I want to tell you anyway that I have continued to fight, imperfectly too often, but still continued to fight against every concept I was raised with.

I have learned that to win is to die a little inside and that taking from another is not the way to gain anything — as a matter of fact, I most assuredly lose precious bits of myself.

I have learned that there are more wretched ways to live than there are wretched ways to die. I have learned that while death is almost always beyond our control in regard to timing, and we have little respect for what it signifies, we have the wretched ways we live our lives, it seems, too much in our control and we have even less respect for life.

I miss you. Too often for the wrong reasons.

The exhilaration of battle and combat. The ecstasy of living and of having taken the life of another. How horribly and sadly misplaced. Rather than celebrating the opportunity to live and progress we glorify the destruction of another and we wallow in that place of self-induced sickness. Lusting after power in any form, trying to re-create what we once felt.

So blind. So damned blind. Looking for that high at the expense of others and through the experiencing of the physical and material and not recognizing that every such experience subtracts from our life, debases us and takes us further from our professed goals.

Yes. I have learned.

I have learned that what I called courage and bravery was the basic instinct for survival gone awry, led by other humans suffering from the same well-rooted delusions.

I have learned that we too quickly succumb to emotional rationalizations to excuse our hate and lust and greed and intolerance and anger and, and, and ...

I have also learned that I have much to learn.

Reading something, hearing something and even being able to put into my own words does not mean that I have learned. Only by living what I have learned means that I have learned it, and even then I will still not have learned it until I am certain in my heart that I will not readily grab onto the first available temptation to regress.

I have known for a very long time that I had no guilt about your death. Now there is not even regret, if there ever was.

But there is regret, sorrow and guilt. One could easily say that has to do more with my life than your death.

Perhaps, in truth, yours was the better path and only those still locked to the material and physical and mental would dare be stupid and low enough to dispute it because they least of all understand. As I did not.

Author's Afterword

Books don't just change readers, they can change their writers. I never imagined that meeting and working with a man who had killed people, sexually abused women and girls, and is an alcoholic would be good for me.

It was.

Perhaps because I met Sam after he had moved from certain darkness into light, I didn't feel alarmed or repulsed; instead, I liked him from the minute we met on a sunny summer morning in a roadside café near a river town. On that day, and over the months we talked, usually in person, sometimes on the phone, I felt a kind of empathetic thrum.

When the phone rang in my office a month before I met Sam, a man on the other end said he needed a writer — not for his own biography but for that of someone he'd met, someone with a story he felt warranted telling, a man we call Sam.

I felt like a detective getting that call, and my imagination flooded with questions to be answered once we met: this guy did what? How did he change? Why? Is that kind of transformation even possible, or is he a con artist of some sort? This book answers those and other questions I did not anticipate.

Sitting with Sam and listening to his thoughts was often if not always unnerving, not for fear of any criminal behavior, but because being with a person attempting to practice radical honesty is rare, and it is discomfiting. As a journalist, it's "the intimacy of truth," to use a phrase from one of his letters, that deep and disciplined candor that make Sam's way of seeing and speaking ideal for my work.

Then there are the PAGGLES, as Sam calls pride, anger, greed, gluttony, lust, envy, and sloth. He hammers at those in himself daily, and I soon found myself doing likewise.

Sam writes — a habit since his service in Vietnam — and his epistles started arriving in my mailbox almost immediately. Some were personal letters to me, many were copies of letters he sends *en masse*, sharing his thoughts, the pages bordered with comic strips, jokes, editorial cartoons, epigrams, and adages clipped from newspapers, forming a sort of decorative stationery.

What I had heard of Sam's life promised to reveal a fascinating if unconventional route and, as I got to know him, an uncommon conclusion: redemption and the growth of his soul. He emphasized that he wanted to get beyond the events of his life — his lost-ness — to spirituality, to epiphanies.

"I never had an epiphany until later years when, incrementally, I realized this ain't been working for me — one more divorce, being drunk, jail," he said. "Everything's gotta be on the table."

Real life and death struggles happen for some under fire in jungles or deserts, and some also take place between dusk and dawn, alone or in cells, bereft of parents or friends, when there is nothing and no one and no consolation. He experienced them all.

About four or five months into writing and interviewing Sam, I was mulling over something writer Anais Nin said "We do not see things as they are, we see things as *we* are," when one of Sam's business-size envelopes arrived. At the bottom of the page Sam denounced humanity, which in his view largely has "No internal grasp of spirituality first as a starting point therefore endless habitual pursuit, emphasis on event telling, endless purposelessness be it yapping in a bar or speechifying to an audience even with good purpose…" followed by the same Nin quote.

This was not the first or last time I would think something, and Sam would say it or mention it in a letter.

While Sam was in Vietnam, I was a college student studying philosophy, eastern religion, and literature, and taking part in anti-war marches. We both saw the futility and destructiveness of the war, one of us at ground level. Later I took my master's degree exam on William James's *The Varieties of Religious Experience, A Study in Human Nature*, which he read in prison, declaring in his typical direct style, "Him and Joseph Campbell — you can shit-can every other book in the world except those."

We grew up in similar small Midwestern farm towns at roughly the same time, and we each have benefitted from more than 20 years of 12 Step programs. Near the top of both our lists of favorite books is Mark Twain's *The Mysterious Stranger*, a critique of organized religion, so we had much to discuss in addition to his life.

During another conversation, Sam expressed doubt that his story could be told effectively or from a spiritual perspective. He did not want his story to be a "series of titillating episodes," he said. "If we don't get to the spiritual change, the basis of it, then it's just a story about a guy who did some dirty things."

"If my real purpose now is to be visionary, and I participate in something that is not, it's a waste of trees for the paper, and I have not done the spiritually right thing," he said. "How do you give some substance to a reader who can take it away and say this is how it works, instead of just telling somebody 'yes, it can'?"

Sam challenged me to go the heart of the matter: what helps you personally identify yourself on a new spiritual basis that no one can ever take from you? The people in his recovery meetings are one answer for him, and he regularly tells me, "The stories I read in recovery books — my role models are those kinds of people. I don't see the black woman or the abandoned child, I see worldly journey and spiritual resolution."

In addition to books and friends in recovery, Sam takes inspiration from films.

"That movie *The Bucket List*, when Jack Nicholson is sitting in the car out in the street watching his granddaughter, I just want to die. I know how much I gave away and what it cost. It's a helluva price to pay."

Two Jim Carrey movies get to him as well.

"*Bruce Almighty,* when he gets to play God for a week and later comes around to where he's supposed to be. And *The Grinch*, I bawl like a baby before it is over."

Above all, Sam is moved by *Saving Private Ryan*, so I checked out the DVD from the library up the block, and as I watched the opening battle sequence, I thought of this now elderly man, sipping oxygen in a small house in a tiny midwestern town, crying out to God, bewailing his own and all human violence, stupidity, venality, and cruelty. At the end of a long session one day, we were sitting in his office and Sam was recalling scenes from the film. He leaned back in his chair and murmured something, and I leaned forward the better to hear him.

"Sam, what did you say?"

"At the beginning and at the end, Ryan is at the military cemetery, and he asks his wife, 'Tell me I'm a good man.' That's what I want most of all, most of all… I want to be a good man."

During the year we've been talking, things have changed and not changed at his home. Sam's model ships no longer sail around his living room — he has given them to me. They now sail on my windowsill and fireplace mantel.

"I'm thinking about getting a cat," he tells me by way of justification. "The cat would just knock the ships over and wreck 'em."

The old green thermos always stands full and hot on the kitchen table, the refrigerator contains a large selection of non-alcoholic beverages, the stack of empty ice cream pails on the kitchen counter has swollen higher, and here are two — two! — bags of chocolate and peanut bars in the 'fridge as well, testimony to one of Sam's worldly weaknesses yet unconquered.

"I had bag of broccoli for lunch," he confesses, as we fantasize about chocolate together. "Don't tell anybody, it will ruin my reputation."

When I break from the kitchen table and head into the kitchen for the cream for my coffee, I see his refrigerator indeed has had a radical transformation. Sam is no longer living on cold ham sandwiches. It is now inhabited by apples and vegetables, and there are pounds and pounds of bagged cheese curds, which he sends home with me at the end of nearly every visit.

He is also smoking less — only one break this time in our three-hour conversation yet he is still, to his disgust, smoking. He may have said he is ready to meet his maker, yet he is obviously trying to stay alive.

When Sam's phone rings, no matter the time of day, he always answers with "Good morning." People come and go; nobody knocks. He is some kind of community hub, offering storage space in his garage or house for someone who is between addresses. He mails books to friends and ships a storm of envelopes. One day he breaks off our talk to speak privately with a couple who come to his kitchen looking grey with worry.

His friendship with others, especially with Martello, continues to grow. It is steady and even understatedly tender. The two correspond regularly via handprinted letters, and Sam tucks in copies of the sermons from my Congregational church.

"He'll never get out, and he doesn't have

anybody," Sam explains to me. He has arranged to provide for Martello after his own death, "He has a blank check with me,"he says.

"What are your favorite colors, Karin?" Sam asked me one day during one of our phone calls. Thinking he's about to give me something, I tell him blue and white.

"Good, because Martello wants to make you an afghan," Sam explains. "Guys in prison really need a goal or something to look forward to and do. He made me one already and now he wants to send you one. It is an opportunity for him to feel like he participates in life. Think of a horse never out of the stall, a cat or dog fed and watered and never out of the cage."

I am surprised and pleased at the idea of someone as formerly dangerous as Martello gently knitting a warm blanket for me, someone he has never met and probably never will.

"Karin, can you identify with my story?" Sam asked me one day when we were taping a multi-hour interview.

"Hell, yes," I replied, swearing being another trait we share.

It's withdrawal during early childhood, and for similar reasons, that we have in common. That and a refusal to ask for help, a determination to do everything alone. I was rescued by animals and nature. Sam was not rescued, and, as a man, he acted out his pain in ways acceptable to his gender — war, killing in battle, drinking, promiscuity — and in unacceptable, even unspeakable actions.

He sometimes does not answer my phone calls, and then I worry, knowing he has been hospitalized more than once for breathing problems.

"I am accepting of my self-limitations now, my health," he says. "I feel an obligation to keep up copying puzzles for prisoners, maintaining the recovery meetings, having a spiritual lifestyle like some of our leaders. I can't take a trip again, but if I could lay my hands on a carpenter bus with a bathroom, I'd be tempted."

On this spring morning, a truck is parked out front, and the driver and his adult son are visiting in Sam's kitchen.

"This is my role model, this is the gentle giant," says Sam, gazing frankly upward and glowing at the tall, sturdy man in denim. The visitor has massive hands and the look of a farmer or mechanic or both. "He and his wife take in small children who need a safe place. I'm envious of him, the opportunity to be with a vulnerable, needy child who needs somebody good in their life. I am never gonna to have that again. I miss the opportunity to be more in my life in ways I can't be."

Sam likes to picture himself as a sort of faulty monk, and he is amused to know that when I studied Buddhism at college, the visiting Japanese *sensei* (teacher) advised us at the end of semester party, "Drink beer! Be happy!"

It would be too simplistic to say this lost man is now both found and happy, but he has attained some redemptive goodness. And he is sticking to what works for him.

The father and son appear to need more time with Sam, and even more people arrive through the open door, I've had too much of that powerful thermos coffee, and it's time to roll. A quick hug and I am off, with Sam saying what he always says instead of good-bye, "Be careful out there."

Sam by Mike Ricci

For a number of years my mother was struggling with her memory and had fallen into dementia. As she slid into Alzheimer's, I watched my father take on the new demands of her care. As they moved from their house of 30 years into different care arrangements, I witnessed a level of love and concern that I didn't think was possible.

On the work front, as a wealth manager, I learned that within six months a brain tumor would take the life of one of my favorite clients. He was more than a client, he was a friend, and I thought about his generous life and how much he loved his family.

"Mike," he would say, "I'm just a dumb guy from the east side, and everything I have in life I owe to God."

We talked about how lucky we both were and how, "Maybe these are the good old days." He always reminded me to be thankful and "Never forget that God makes all of this possible."

It was through these struggles that I began to wonder what life was truly about. I asked myself, "What is it we are here to do? What is my purpose, and what is it that I am supposed to be doing?"

I came to learn that these are the big questions we start to ask ourselves as we approach 50, and I was following the playbook like so many others before me.

During this time, and as a member of my church finance council, I was asked to visit the Catholic Community Foundation of Minnesota, the organization responsible for managing the endowment of our parish.

I discussed our parish account and visited with some key leadership people at the foundation, who told me a new professional outreach position was being formulated. I was asked to consider it.

The outreach job would entail working with other wealth advisors, accountants, and attorneys to create awareness about the benefits of the foundation and allow professionals to direct more clients in giving.

Over time, I began to ponder the idea of actually making a change. It would be a big step for me and my family, as I was arguably entering the peak earnings potential period of my career. My wife was supportive of a change and said we should pray on it, and God would show us the way.

One day my phone rang, and it was Joe, a client.

"Mike, I have a friend who has some money, but doesn't know what he's doing," he said. "Will you meet with him?"

I agreed.

"You need to know that I met this man when he was in prison," said Joe. "At the time, I was volunteering as a member of Amicus, a group that connects citizens with prisoners."

I wasn't going to turn down a referral and agreed to visit his friend.

We set up a morning coffee meeting at a Perkins. He wore a blue Vietnam baseball cap with various medals pinned on the front, and he smelled like a pack of cigarettes. We sat down for a cup of coffee, and he said in a deep, raspy voice, "If Joe trusts you, then I trust you."

"Good, so if we are going to work together, I'll need you to give me full disclosure," I told him.

He nodded slowly and looked out the window and, being a man of little financial experience or understanding, turned back to me and slowly said, "Okay, I'll give you full disclosure."

He folded his hands together on the table and started by saying, "I want you to know that I believe in God."

As he spoke, I could see tears begin to well up in his eyes, and he pressed on, "I want you to know that God doesn't make junk or wasted souls." Then he paused and looked out the window again to gather himself so his voice would not crack, and he added, "We waste too much time in our culture on things that don't matter, you see… there's just not enough love."

I have done hundreds of prospect meetings during my career, and never once did they start like this.

I spent the next two and half hours listening to his story, his full disclosure, and, in the back of my mind, I knew that this was not a chance meeting. It seemed to me we had been brought together through a higher power, and that he was a special man with an important message. When he began to explain that he was going to inherit some money and that he wanted to "give it all away," I could feel the angels surrounding us.

"I don't want to give all the money away right away," he said "I want to open an account that I can name after the only people who loved me and cared for me. I want to stay anonymous, and I want this account to grow and give every year forever in their names to honor and remember them."

He was describing the essence of an endowment, a tool foundations use to promote lifetime giving, and he was doing this without any real understanding of money or finance. Then he reached out and put his hand on my arm and said, "Can you help me with this? Will you help me with this?"

At that moment, I realized my prayer was being answered and that it would be okay for me to make a career change. I had been brought together with a new friend, one who would open my eyes to a new path that was indeed possible, a friend whose journey and story was his gift to me and, now, to you.

My hope for you, dear reader, is simple.

We are given many gifts, and we all travel different paths. Some of us face great hardship in our lives, and some of us are blessed at birth and never know what hardship really is. Some of us find faith in a higher power, others do not believe at all.

Ask yourself, "Am I thankful for what I have been given? Am I generous with the gifts I have received? Do I truly know pain and suffering, or could I help those who have been less fortunate? Am I spiritual? Am I growing my soul?"

Life is short and precious, and your time on earth will be fleeting. Don't waste it on things that do not matter. As Sam says, there's just not enough love.

— M

Proceeds from the sales of this book go to Sam's endowment, managed by the Catholic Community Foundation of Minnesota to honor those who loved him and to support causes dear to him.

Acknowledgements

Thanks to: Laurel O'Neill for her diligent professional transcription and listening to the hard stuff; Joan Nygren for book design and consultation; Kit Naylor for copyediting and wielding a wicked Oxford comma; to Wendy Waiwaiole for giving the manuscript the in-depth reading it needed and making it a better, clearer book. Laurie Schneider not only provided the photo, as usual, but intermittent tech advice and kept me supplied at home to keep writing. Lynn Dosch brought her skills and empathy as a professional storyteller and grief group leader. Carol Parry tended to my needs so I could get this finished and offered kind critique. Sally Nettleton brought wisdom, insight and affirmation. Stan and Connie Suchta served as my two-person test reading group of devout Catholics. My gratitude as always to fellow journalist and author Carol Pine for project consultation and leading the way.

Thanks to members of the Ricci family including Michael A. Ricci, Sr. for their support, assistance and patience, and suggestions.

Our gratitude as well to Valentina Plant, Bruce Nygren, and Ruben Rosario.

About The Author

Karin Winegar is a St. Paul, Minnesota-based journalist and author. A graduate of Carleton College and the University of Minnesota, she was a staff writer at the *Minneapolis Star Tribune* for 20 years.

She specializes in writing, editing, and producing life stories through biographies and luxury privately commissioned volumes.

Her book *"SAVED, Rescued Animals and the Lives They Transform"* (Perseus/Da Capo) features photography by Judy Olausen, a foreword by Dr. Jane Goodall and a preface by Dr. Temple Grandin.

She has won numerous honors, including Lowell Thomas awards for investigative reporting and for maritime journalism. Her work has appeared in *The New York Times, The Wall Street Journal, The Los Angeles Times, Condé Nast Traveler, Bon Appetit, Cowboys & Indians, Better Homes and Gardens, Mother Jones, PEOPLE, The Utne Reader, Corporate Report, The Washington Post, San Francisco Examiner, SAILING, Cruising World, Western Horseman, American Quarter Horse Journal, EQUUS, Practical Horseman,* and *Horse & Rider,* among others.

Information and samples of her work can be seen at www.karinwinegar.com